Nikon®
D3000
Digital Field Guide

Nikon®
D3000
Digital Field Guide

J. Dennis Thomas

WILEY

Wiley Publishing, Inc.

Nikon® D3000 Digital Field Guide

Published by
Wiley Publishing, Inc.
10475 Crosspoint Boulevard
Indianapolis, IN 46256
www.wiley.com

WILEY

About the Author

J. Dennis Thomas is a freelance photographer and author based out of Austin, Texas. He has nearly 25 years of experience behind the lenses of Nikon cameras. His work has been published in many regional and national publications including *Rolling Stone* and *SXSW World* magazines. He has written ten highly successful *Digital Field Guides* for Wiley publishing with more in the works.

Credits

Acquisitions Editor
Courtney Allen

Executive Editor
Jody Lefevere

Project Editor
Jama Carter

Technical Editor
Ben Holland

Senior Copy Editor
Kim Heusel

Editorial Director
Robyn Siesky

Editorial Manager
Cricket Krengel

Business Manager
Amy Knies

Senior Marketing Manager
Sandy Smith

Vice President and Executive Group Publisher
Richard Swadley

Vice President and Executive Publisher
Barry Pruett

Project Coordinator
Kristie Rees

Graphics and Production Specialists
Jennifer Mayberry
Ronald Terry

Quality Control Technician
Melanie Hoffman

Proofreading and Indexing
Linda Seifert
BIM Indexing & Proofreading Services

Acknowledgments

Thanks to Cricket, Courtney, Jama, Sarah, Laura, and everyone else at Wiley. Muchas gracias to all the folks at Precision Camera in Austin, Texas.

Contents

CHAPTER 3
Exploring the Nikon D3000 Menus 59

CHAPTER 6
Working with Light   131

CHAPTER 7
Real World Applications 159

APPENDIX C
**How to Use the Gray Card and
Color Checker   231**

Glossary   233

Index   240

Introduction

Welcome to the *Nikon D3000 Digital Field Guide*. This book is a handy reference for you to get started learning about all of the features and functions of your Nikon D3000 dSLR camera.

This *Digital Field Guide* isn't meant to replace the user's manual but to be an adjunct to it, explaining things more simply and in more detail than in the manual. The guide is aimed at D3000 owners who are just beginning in the world of digital SLRs up to advanced users with more hands-on knowledge of photography.

The *Nikon D3000 Digital Field Guide* covers not only the specifics of the D3000 but also many other facets of digital photography, from the basics of exposure to lighting and composition. There's also a chapter to help you get started with Nikon's Creative Lighting System and all of the possibilities that Nikon's Speedlights offer.

About This Book

The first few chapters cover the basics of the camera: the buttons and switches, the menu options, and the different settings. These are all described in detail with some tips on how to effectively use them.

Other chapters include information on lenses, how they work, and what applications specific lenses are best for. There's a primer on working with different lighting types as well as a chapter that teaches you how to take on different photographic tasks.

To put it simply, there's a lot of information in this book. There's a good bit of information for everyone, from the new photographer to the advanced hobbyist.

About the D3000

The D3000 is Nikon's newest (and smallest) entry-level camera and has much in common with the popular D5000. Basically what Nikon did was cut out all of the bells and whistles of the D5000 to produce a powerful camera that is extremely simple to operate even for the most inexperienced of photographers.

The D3000 has something that no other entry-level Nikon dSLR has, the Multi-CAM 1000 autofocus (AF) module that was introduced with Nikon's semiprofessional D200. This is a very fast and accurate AF module that allows you more precise control of focus than you could get with previous models. The D3000 also has 3D-tracking focus, which makes it a snap for shooting pictures of moving subjects without worrying about focus.

The D3000 has the Scene modes that make it simple to shoot in almost any situation as well as the more hands-on Manual and semiautomatic (Shutter and Aperture Priority) modes that are available on all professional cameras.

The Retouch menu allows you to do all of your editing in-camera using the big 3-inch LCD monitor. This allows you to process your pictures without ever touching a computer!

Nikon has made the D3000 available with the highly touted 18-55mm f/3.5-5.6 VR. This is a great all-around lens that covers the most used focal lengths. From the moderately wide 18mm to use for architecture, interiors, and landscapes to 55mm, which is perfect for portraits, this lens covers most of your basic photography needs. The added bonus of Nikon's Vibration Reduction allows you to hand hold the camera at slower shutter speeds without worrying about blurry pictures caused by camera shake. The Silent Wave motor in the lens allows for quick, nearly silent focusing.

Another great thing about the D3000 is that, like all other Nikon SLRs, you can use almost all lenses manufactured by Nikon in the last 75 years, albeit some of them will have limited functionality. Nikon is known for having some of the highest quality optics in the industry.

One thing is for sure, you will be enjoying your camera for many years to come and with some help from this book, you will gain a deeper knowledge not only of your camera, but of photography as well.

Quick Tour

The Quick Tour is designed to cover the basic functions you need to know to get you started using your D3000 right away. If you've already used a Nikon dSLR, a lot of this may be familiar to you. In fact, if you upgraded from a D60, the setup for the D3000 is very similar. If you are upgrading from a compact digital camera, you probably should read the entire Quick Tour to familiarize yourself with the camera layout.

This Quick Tour assumes that you have already unpacked the camera, read the manual, charged the batteries, mounted a lens, and inserted the memory card. If you haven't done these things, do them now.

I'm sure you're ready to get out there and shoot some photos with your new D3000, so let's get going.

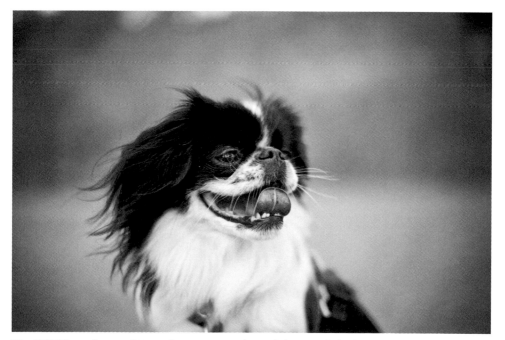

The D3000 can be used to grab awesome shots right out of the box.

Selecting a Shooting Mode

If you're anything like me, I'm sure you're ready to get out there and start taking pictures with your new camera. The great thing about the D3000 is that you can start taking great photos right out of the box. The D3000 has some automatic shooting modes that choose the proper settings for you. All you really have to do is point the camera at something and shoot!

The first thing you need to do is turn the camera on. The on/off switch is located right on top of the camera surrounding the Shutter Release button.

Changing the shooting mode is simple: rotate the Mode dial located on the top of the camera. The shooting mode is also shown on the top-left corner of the LCD when the shooting info is displayed.

The D3000 has quite a few Shooting modes. It has four standard shooting modes: P, S, A, and M. In addition to these modes, the D3000 also employs Scene modes. These are modes that apply settings that are optimized to the type of scene you're shooting. These include modes for shooting portraits, sports, children, and a few others.

The D3000 has what is termed by Nikon as a Guide menu. This menu option walks you through the different Shooting modes as well as viewing and deleting images and camera setup. Because the Guide mode is pretty self-explanatory and is made to guide you through all the options, I'm not going to give it much coverage in this book.

The scene and Auto modes include the following:

▶ **Auto.** This is a "point-and-shoot" mode in which the camera controls all the settings including shutter speed, aperture, and ISO. If the camera deems it necessary, the built-in flash automatically activates.

▶ **Auto (flash off).** This setting is similar to the Auto mode; the camera controls all settings. However, in this mode, the flash is disabled. This is a good setting to use when natural lighting is preferred or the use of flash is not allowed (such as in a museum).

▶ **Portrait.** This mode uses a wider aperture allowing the background to be soft while giving you sharp focus on your subject.

▶ **Landscape.** This mode chooses a smaller aperture to ensure that focus is achieved throughout the image. The camera also enhances blues and greens to accentuate the sky and foliage in the scene.

► **Child.** This setting optimizes skin tones and boosts the saturation a bit for more vivid colors.

► **Sports.** With this setting the camera chooses a higher shutter speed to freeze the action.

► **Close Up.** This setting provides sharp details on the subject while allowing the background to soften to draw attention to the subject.

► **Night Portrait.** This setting uses flash to capture your subject while maintaining a longer shutter speed to capture the ambient light of the background resulting in an evenly balanced more natural looking exposure.

The scene modes take care of all the settings for you, including activating the flash. These modes are handy when starting out, but you are limited in fine-tuning the settings. Once you get more familiar with the camera settings such as aperture and shutter speed, you may find yourself eschewing these scene modes in favor of choosing the more flexible modes of P, S, A, or M.

The D3000 has four standard shooting modes.

► **P.** Also known as Programmed Auto mode. This is a fully automatic shooting mode in which the camera decides both the aperture setting and shutter speed. You can use the Command dial to adjust the aperture and shutter to better suit your needs. This is known as Flexible Program, and it allows you to control the settings while maintaining the same exposure. Use this mode when taking snapshots. You can let the camera control all your settings, but you can also use the Flexible Program if you need. This gives you the best of both worlds.

Image courtesy of Nikon, Inc.

QT.1 Rotate the Mode dial to select a Shooting mode.

► **S.** Also known as Shutter Priority mode. This is a semiautomatic mode in which you decide the shutter speed to use and the camera chooses the appropriate aperture. Use this mode when you need fast shutter speeds to freeze action or slow shutter speeds to show motion blur. Be sure not to use this mode when you need to control the amount of the image that is in focus.

▶ **A.** Also known as Aperture Priority mode. This is another semiautomatic mode where you adjust the aperture to control how much of the image is in focus (the depth of field). Use this mode when you want to isolate a subject by focusing on it and letting the background go soft, or if you want to be sure that everything in the picture is in sharp focus.

▶ **M.** Also known as Manual mode. With this mode, you decide the shutter speed and aperture. You can use this mode when you want to completely control the exposure in order to achieve a certain tonality in your image by purposefully over- or underexposing the image. To help you when using this mode, you can check the D3000 light meter in the viewfinder.

Focusing

Your Nikon D3000 camera can automatically focus on the subject when using the lens that comes with the D3000 kit. The lens that comes with the D3000 kit is the AF-S DX Nikkor 18-55mm f/3.5-5.6G VR. This lens can be focused automatically or manually. To use the autofocus (AF) feature you must first be sure that the switch on the lens is set to A.

Image courtesy of Nikon, Inc.

QT.2 The A/M switch on the kit lens

Auto-focusing the camera is done simply by pressing the Shutter Release button halfway. The focus areas that are used to determine focus are shown in the viewfinder as a series of 11 brackets. One or more of these brackets will momentarily light up in red when the camera achieves focus.

By default, the camera automatically focuses on the closest subject in all modes except for the Close-Up mode in which the camera uses the center focus point or Sports DVP mode in which the camera uses all focus points to help track the subject.

Once the camera locks focus, a small green light in the bottom-left corner of the viewfinder lights up. If you want to lock focus and exposure settings, you can press the Auto-Exposure/Autofocus Lock (AE-L/AF-L) button that is found to the right of the viewfinder. This allows you to recompose your photo while maintaining the focus and exposure readings on your subject.

Once the camera achieves focus, all you need to do is press down fully on the Shutter Release button to take your picture.

Playback

After you shoot some images with your D3000, you can look at them on the big bright 3-inch LCD screen. To view your images, press the Play button on the top rear of the camera to the left of the viewfinder. The most recent photo taken is the first image displayed. You can use the Multi-selector left or right to scroll through the images or up or down to check the settings and histograms.

To scroll through the images that are stored on the SD card, press the Multi-selector button left or right. Pressing the button to the right allows you to view the images in the sequence that they were taken. Pressing the button to the left displays the images in reverse order.

There are a few other options available to you when the camera is in Playback mode:

▶ **Press the Thumbnail/Zoom out button to view thumbnails.** You can choose to view either 4, 9, or 72 images at a time, and you can also view the thumbnails in a calendar view. When in Thumbnail mode, use the Multi-selector to navigate among the thumbnails to highlight one. You can then press the OK button to bring the selected image to a full-size preview.

▶ **Press the Zoom in button to magnify the image.** This button allows you to check for sharpness or look for details. Pressing this button also takes you out of the thumbnail preview.

▶ **Press the Protect button to save images from being deleted.** The Protect button (denoted by a key) locks the image to prevent you from accidentally erasing it when editing your images in the camera.

 When the memory card is formatted, all images including the protected ones are erased.

▶ **Use the Multi-selector to view image data.** To check to see what settings were used when the photograph was taken, press the Multi-selector up or down. This also allows you to check the histogram, which is a visual representation of the tonality of the image.

▶ **Press the OK button to do in-camera photo editing.** Pressing the OK button displays a menu that allows you to do some rudimentary in-camera editing such as D-Lighting, fixing red-eye, and cropping.

 For more detailed information on in-camera editing, see Chapter 8.

▶ **Press the Delete button to erase images.** The Delete button has an icon shaped like a trashcan on it. Press this button to permanently erase the image from your memory card. When the Delete button is pressed, the camera asks for confirmation. Press the Delete button again to complete the deletion.

Menu button

Playback button

Protect button

Zoom in/Info button

Delete button | Multi-selector

Thumbnail/Zoom out button

OK button

Image courtesy of Nikon, Inc.

QT.3 These buttons can be used in the Playback mode for a variety of functions.

 For more detailed information on settings, see Chapter 2 for modes and Chapter 3 for menu settings.

Downloading

When you fill up a card or you're ready to do some post-processing of your images, you want to download them off of your SD card and onto your computer for storage. You can either download the images straight from the camera to your computer or you can remove the memory card from the camera and use a card reader to transfer the images.

To download from the camera using the USB cable, follow these steps:

1. **Turn off the camera.** Be sure that the camera is off when connecting it to the computer to ensure that the camera's or computer's electronics are not damaged.

2. **Open the rubber cover that conceals the D3000's output connections.** On the left side of the camera with the back facing you is a cover that has the camera's USB and Video out ports.

3. **Connect the camera to the USB cable.** Your D3000 comes wwith a USB cable. Plug the small end of the cable into the camera and plug the other end into a USB slot on your computer.

4. **Turn the camera on.** Once turned on, your computer should recognize the camera as a mass storage device. You can then drag and drop your files or you can use a software program, such as Adobe Bridge or Nikon Transfer, to transfer your files.

To download using a card reader, follow these steps:

1. **Turn off the camera.** Be sure that the camera is off and the memory card access lamp (the small green LED near the card door) isn't blinking before removing the card.

2. **Remove the memory card.** Open the memory card door cover and press the SD card in to eject it.

3. **Insert the SD card into the card reader.** Be sure that the reader is connected to your computer. Your computer should recognize the card as a mass storage device, and you can drag and drop the files or you can use a software program, such as Adobe Bridge or Nikon View, to transfer your files.

 Depending on your software and how your computer is set up, your computer may offer to automatically transfer the files to a predetermined destination.

CHAPTER 1

Exploring the Nikon D3000

This chapter covers the key components of the Nikon D3000. These are the features that are most readily accessible because they are situated on the outside of the camera: the buttons, knobs, switches, and dials.

If you are upgrading from another dSLR, some of this will likely be a review, but there are some new features that you may or may not be aware of, so a quick read through is a good idea even if you are an experienced Nikon dSLR user.

For those of you who may be just beginning into the world of dSLRs, this chapter is a great way to get acquainted with some of the terms that are used in conjunction with your new camera.

So fasten your seatbelts, and get ready to explore the D3000!

Getting to know all your camera's menus, buttons, and dials allows you to quickly change your settings so you don't miss a shot.

Key Components of the D3000

If you've read the Quick Tour, you should be pretty familiar with the basic buttons and switches that you need to do the basic settings. In this section, you look at the camera from all sides and break down the layout so that you know what everything on the surface of the camera does.

This section doesn't cover the menus, only the exterior controls. Although there are many features you can access with just the push of a button, oftentimes you can change the same setting inside of a menu option. Although the D3000 doesn't have the same amount of buttons as some of its bigger siblings in the Nikon line, it does have quite a few of them. Knowing exactly what these buttons do can save you loads of time and help you to not miss out on getting a shot.

Top of the camera

The top of the D3000 is where you find some of the most important buttons and dials. This is where you can change the Shooting mode and press the Shutter Release button to take your photo. Also included in this section is a brief description of some of the things you will find on the top of the lens. Although your lens may vary, most of the features are quite similar from lens to lens.

▶ **Shutter Release button.** In my opinion, this is the most important button on the camera. Halfway pressing this button activates the camera's autofocus and light meter. When you fully depress this button, the shutter is released and a photograph is taken. When the camera has been idle and has "gone to sleep," lightly pressing the Shutter Release button wakes up the camera. When the image review is on, lightly pressing the Shutter Release button turns off the LCD and prepares the camera for another shot.

▶ **On/Off switch.** This switch, located around the Shutter Release button, is used to turn the camera on and off. Push the switch all the way to the left to turn off the camera. Pull the switch to the right to turn your camera on.

▶ **Mode dial.** This is an important dial. Rotating this dial allows you to quickly change your shooting mode. You can choose one of the scene modes, one of the semiautomatic modes, or you can choose to set the exposure manually. For a detailed description of all of the exposure modes, see Chapter 2.

▶ **Info button.** Pressing this button brings up the Information Display (Info display), which is discussed in more detail later in this chapter.

Focal length indicators

Zoom ring

Focus ring

On/Off switch

Hot shoe   Mode dial

Info button

Shutter Release button
Exposure compensation/
Aperture button

Focal plane mark

Image courtesy of Nikon, Inc.

1.1 Top-of-the-camera controls

▶ **Exposure compensation/Aperture button.** Pressing this button in conjunction with spinning the Command dial allows you to modify the exposure that is set by the D3000's light meter when set to P, S, or A mode. Turning the Command

11

dial to the right decreases exposure while turning the dial to the left increases the exposure. This button also doubles as the Aperture button when the camera is set to Manual exposure mode. Pressing the button while rotating the Command dial allows you to adjust your lens aperture. Additionally, when pressing this button in conjunction with the Flash mode, you can adjust your Flash Exposure Compensation by rotating the Command dial.

The Exposure compensation/Aperture button serves no functions when shooting in the automatic or scene modes.

▶ **Focal plane mark.** The focal plane mark shows you where the plane of the image sensor is inside the camera. The sensor is directly behind the lens opening. When doing certain types of photography, particularly macro photography using a bellows lens, you need to measure the length of the bellows from the front element of the lens to the focal plane. This is where the focal plane mark comes in handy.

▶ **Hot shoe.** This is where an accessory flash is attached to the camera body. The hot shoe has an electronic contact that tells the flash to fire when the shutter is released. There are also a number of other electronic contacts that allow the camera to communicate with the flash to enable the automated features of a dedicated flash unit such as the SB-600.

▶ **Focus ring.** Rotating the focus ring allows you to focus the lens manually. The location of the focus ring varies by lens. With old AF (non AF-S) lenses, and even older manual focus lenses, just turn the ring to focus the lens. With newer AF-S lenses, such as the kit lens, there's a switch on the lens labeled "A" and "M". Select M before attempting to manually focus. If you don't switch it over first, you can damage the lens. Some higher end AF-S lenses have a switch labeled "A/M" and "M". With these lenses set to the A/M position, you can manually override the autofocus at any time without damaging the lens.

For more information on lenses and compatibility, see Chapter 5.

▶ **Zoom ring.** Rotating the zoom ring allows you to change the focal length of the lens. Prime lenses do not have a zoom ring.

▶ **Focal length indicators.** These numbers indicate which focal length in millimeters your lens is zoomed to.

Back of the camera

The back of the camera is where you find the buttons that mainly control playback and menu options, although there are a few buttons that control some of the shooting functions. Most of the buttons have more than one function — a lot of them are used in conjunction with the Command dial or the Multi-selector. On the back of the camera you also find several key features, including the all-important viewfinder and LCD.

▶ **LCD.** This is the most obvious feature on the back of the camera. This big 3-inch, 230,000-dot liquid crystal display (LCD) screen is a very bright, high-resolution screen. The LCD is where you view all your current camera settings as well as review your images after shooting.

▶ **Viewfinder.** This is what you look through to compose your photographs. Light coming through the lens is reflected from a series of five mirrors (called a pentamirror) enabling you to see exactly what you're shooting. Around the viewfinder is a rubber eyepiece that serves to give you a softer place to rest your eye and to block any extra light from entering the viewfinder as you compose and shoot your images.

▶ **Diopter adjustment control.** Just to the right of the viewfinder (hidden behind the eyecup) is the Diopter adjustment control. Use this control to adjust the viewfinder lens to suit your individual vision differences (not everyone's eyesight is the same). To adjust this, look through the viewfinder, and press the Shutter Release button halfway to focus on something. If what you see in the viewfinder isn't quite sharp, slide the Diopter adjustment up or down until everything appears in focus. The manual warns you not to put your finger or fingernail in your eye. I agree that this might not be a good idea.

▶ **AE-L/AF-L/Protect.** The Auto-Exposure/Autofocus lock button is used to lock the Auto-Exposure (AE) and Autofocus (AF). When in Playback mode this button can be pressed to lock an image to protect it from being deleted. A small key icon will be displayed in the upper left-hand corner of images that are protected. This button can be customized to provide AE Lock only, AF Lock only, AE Lock (hold), or AF-ON. AE Lock (hold) locks the exposure with one press of the button; the exposure is locked until the button is pressed again or the shutter is released. AF-ON engages the AF in the same way that half-pressing the shutter does.

▶ **Command dial.** This dial is used to change a variety of settings depending on which button you are using in conjunction with it. By default, it is used to change the shutter speed when in Shutter Priority and Manual mode or the aperture when in Aperture Priority. It is also used to adjust exposure compensation and change the flash mode.

► **Multi-selector.** The Multi-selector is another button that serves a few different purposes. In Playback mode the Multi-selector is used to scroll through the photographs you've taken, and it can also be used to view image information such as histograms and shooting settings. When in certain Shooting modes the Multi-selector can be used to change the active focus point when in Single-point or Dynamic-area AF mode. It also serves to navigate through the menu options.

► **OK button.** When in the Menu mode, press this button to select the menu item that is highlighted.

Menu button   Command dial

Playback button   AE-L/AF-L/Protect button   Multi-selector

Zoom in/Info display button   LCD   Delete button   Ok button

Thumbnail/Zoom out/Help button   Memory card access lamp

Image courtesy of Nikon, Inc.

1.2 Back-of-the-camera controls

▶ **Delete button.** When reviewing your pictures, if you find some that you don't want to keep, you can delete them by pressing this button marked with a trash-can icon. To prevent accidental deletion of images, the camera displays a dialog box asking you to confirm that you want to erase the picture. Press the Delete button a second time to permanently erase the image.

▶ **Memory card access lamp.** This light blinks when the memory card is in use. Under no circumstances should you remove the card when this light is on or blinking. You could damage your card or camera and lose any information in the camera's buffer.

▶ **Playback button.** Pressing this button displays the most recently taken photograph. You can also view other pictures by pressing the Multi-selector left and right.

▶ **Menu button.** Press this button to access the D3000 menu options. There are a number of different menus, including Playback, Shooting, Custom Settings, and Retouch. Use the Multi-selector to choose the menu you want to view.

▶ **Thumbnail/Zoom out/Help button.** In Playback mode, pressing this button allows you to go from full-frame playback (or viewing the whole image) to viewing thumbnails. The thumbnails can be displayed as 4, 9, or 72 images on a page. You can also view images by calendar date. When viewing the menu options, pressing this button displays a help screen that explains the functions of that particular menu option. When in Shooting mode, pressing this button explains the functions of that particular mode. When viewing the Information Display and a flashing question mark appears, you can press this button for help. This button also allows you to zoom out after you have zoomed in on a particular image.

▶ **Zoom in button/Info display button.** When reviewing your images, you can press the Zoom in button to get a closer look at the details of your image. This is a handy feature for checking the sharpness and focus of your shot. When zoomed in, use the Multi-selector to navigate around within the image. To view your other images at the same zoom ratio, you can rotate the Command dial. To return to full-frame playback, press the Zoom out button. You may have to press the Zoom out button multiple times depending on how much you have zoomed in. When the camera is "asleep," pressing this button shows the Info display. When the Info display is shown, pressing this button again gives access to some settings that can be changed. Use the Multi-selector to highlight the desired setting to change, then press the OK button to access the options.

CROSS REF For more detailed information on changing settings in the Info display, see Chapter 3.

Front of the camera

The front of the D3000 (lens facing you) is where you find the buttons to quickly adjust the flash settings as well as some camera focusing options, and with certain lenses you will find some buttons that control focusing and Vibration Reduction (VR).

▶ **Built-in flash.** This option is a handy feature that allows you to take sharp pictures in low-light situations. Although not as versatile as one of the external Nikon Speedlights such as the SB-600 or SB-400, the built-in flash can be used very effectively and is great for snapshots; although I highly recommend getting a flash diffuser if you plan on using it much.

 For more on using flash, see Chapter 6.

AF-assist illuminator   Built-in flash

Infrared receiver

Image courtesy of Nikon, Inc.

1.3 Front of the Nikon D3000

▶ **AF-assist illuminator.** This is an LED that shines on the subject to help the camera to focus when the lighting is dim. The AF-assist illuminator only lights when in Single Focus mode (AF-S) or Automatic Focus mode (AF-A). This is also lit when the camera is set to Red-Eye Reduction flash using the camera's built-in flash.

▶ **Infrared receiver.** This allows you to wirelessly control the camera shutter release using the optional ML-L3 infrared transmitter. The ML-L3 is a great little accessory that costs less than $20. It's one of the best accessories you can get.

Right side

On the right side of the camera (lens facing you) are the output terminals on the D3000. These are used to connect your camera to a computer or to an external source for viewing your images directly from the camera. These terminals are hidden under a plastic cover that helps keep out dust and moisture.

Flash pop-up button/Flash mode button/Flash Exposure Compensation button

Self-timer/Fn (function) button

Lens focus mode selector

Video out

VR switch

USB port

Lens release button

Image courtesy of Nikon, Inc.

1.4 The right side of the D3000

▶ **Flash pop-up button/Flash mode button/Flash Exposure Compensation button.** When using P, S, A, or M exposure modes, press this button to open and activate the built-in Speedlight. Pressing this button and rotating the Command dial on the rear of the camera allows you to choose a flash mode. Depending on the shooting mode you can choose from among Front-Curtain Sync, Red-Eye Reduction, Red-Eye Reduction with Slow Sync, Slow Sync, and Rear-Curtain Sync. Once the flash is popped up, pressing this button in conjunction with the Exposure Compensation button and rotating the Command dial allows you to adjust the Flash Exposure Compensation (FEC). FEC allows you to adjust the flash output to make the flash brighter or dimmer depending on your needs. When shooting in Auto or scene modes, the flash is automatically activated and some Flash sync modes aren't available depending on the scene mode.

- **Auto, Portrait, Child, Close-up.** When using these modes, you can select Auto-flash, Auto with Red-Eye Reduction, or set to Off.

- **Night portrait.** With this mode you can select Auto with Slow Sync and Red-Eye Reduction, Auto with Slow Sync, or set to Off.

- **P, A.** With these modes you can select Fill flash, Red-Eye Reduction, Slow Sync with Red-Eye Reduction, Slow Sync, or Rear Curtain with Slow Sync.

- **S, M.** These modes allow you to use Fill flash, Red-Eye Reduction, or Rear-Curtain Sync.

▶ **Self-timer/Fn (function) button.** By default, pressing this button activates the camera's self-timer. When the self-timer is on, the camera delays the shutter release to allow you to get into the picture or to reduce vibration caused by shaking the camera when pressing the Shutter Release button while the camera is attached to a tripod. This button can also be set to provide other functions. You can set the button to quickly change the release mode, image quality, ISO sensitivity, or white balance via the Info display. Pressing the Fn button and rotating the Command dial changes the settings. You can change the setting in the Setup menu under the Buttons option.

▶ **Lens release button.** This button disengages the locking mechanism of the lens, allowing the lens to be rotated and removed from the lens mount.

▶ **Video out.** This connection, officially called Standard video output, is used to connect the camera to a standard TV or VCR for viewing your images on-screen. The D3000 is connected with the EG-D100 video cable that is available separately from Nikon.

▶ **USB port.** This is where the USB cable plugs in to attach the camera to your computer to transfer images straight from the camera. The USB cable is also used to connect the camera to the computer when using Nikon's optional Camera Control Pro 2 software.

▶ **Lens Focus mode selector.** This switch is used to choose between using the lens in Auto or Manual focus.

▶ **VR switch.** This allows you to turn the Vibration Reduction (VR) on or off. When shooting in normal or bright light it's best to turn the VR off to reduce battery consumption.

Left side

On the left side of the camera (lens facing you) is the memory card slot cover. Sliding this door toward the back of the camera opens it so you can insert or remove your memory card.

Bottom

The bottom of the camera has a couple of features that are quite important.

▶ **Battery chamber cover.** This covers the chamber that holds the EN-EL9a battery that is supplied with your D3000. If you look closely at the battery chamber, there is a small rubber cover that can be moved out of the way to make way for the cord of the EH-5a AC adapter that is available separately from Nikon.

▶ **Tripod socket.** This is where you attach a tripod or monopod to help steady your camera.

Memory card slot cover

Image courtesy of Nikon, Inc.

1.5 Memory card slot cover.

Viewfinder Display

When looking through the viewfinder, you see a lot of useful information about the photo you are setting up. Most of the information is also displayed in the Information Display screen, but it is less handy when you are looking through the viewfinder composing a shot. Here is a complete list of all the information you get from the viewfinder display.

▶ **Framing grid.** This grid is used as an aid in composition. You can use the intersecting lines to compose in the Rule of Thirds and the straight line to line up your compositions. By default the framing grid is turned off, but it can be turned on in the Setup menu under the Viewfinder options heading.

▶ **Center-weighted metering reference.** This circle gives you an idea of how much of the frame is being used to calculate 75 percent of the exposure when using Center-weighted metering.

▶ **No SD card indicator.** When this icon is blinking, there is no card in the slot or the card is locked, inserted improperly, corrupt, or otherwise damaged.

▶ **Battery indicator.** This shows up when the battery is low. When the battery is completely exhausted, this icon blinks and the shutter release is disabled.

▶ **Focus point display.** This shows you which AF point is chosen by showing it with a bracket around it. When set to Auto Area, no AF point is chosen until the camera achieves focus, then one or more AF points will be displayed with brackets.

▶ **Focus indicator.** This is a green dot that lets you know whether the camera detects that the scene is in focus. When focus is achieved, the green dot lights up; if the camera is not in focus, no dot is displayed.

▶ **AE Lock indicator.** When this is lit, you know that the Auto-Exposure Lock button has been pressed. The exposure is now locked and remains so until the button is released.

▶ **Shutter speed display.** This simply shows how long your shutter is set to stay open from 30 seconds (30") up to 1/4000 (4000) second.

▶ **Aperture/f-stop display.** This shows what your current aperture setting is. The words *aperture* and *f/stop* are used interchangeably. Your aperture setting is how wide your lens opening is.

Framing grid

Focus points

Center-weighted metering reference circle

No SD card indicator

Battery indicator

Focus indicator

AE Lock indicator

Flexible program indicator

Shutter speed

Aperture (f/stop)

Exposure indicator/Rangefinder

Warning indicator

Flash ready indicator

Thousands indicator

Remaining exposures/ WB recording/ FEC/EV/ISO

FEC indicator

Auto-ISO indicator

Exposure compensation indicator

1.6 Viewfinder display

▶ **Remaining exposures.** This set of numbers lets you know how many more exposures can fit on the memory card. The actual number of exposures may vary according to file information and compression. When the Shutter Release button is half-pressed, the display changes to show how many exposures can fit in the camera's *buffer* before the buffer is full and the frame rate slows down. The buffer is in-camera RAM that stores your image data while the data is being

21

written to the memory card. This area also indicates that the WB is ready to be set by flashing PRE; it displays the amount of exposure compensation and FEC when the Exposure Compensation button is pressed. The ISO sensitivity is also displayed here when the Fn. button is set to ISO sensitivity.

▶ **K.** This lets you know that there are more than 1,000 exposures remaining on your memory card.

▶ **Flash ready indicator.** When this is displayed, the flash, whether it is the built-in flash or an external Speedlight attached to the hot shoe, is fully charged and ready to fire at full power.

▶ **Flexible Program indicator.** When this is lit, it lets you know that the exposure has been modified from the original settings defined when using the Programmed Auto exposure mode. To return to the default settings, rotate the Command dial until this indicator disappears or simply switch to another exposure mode setting and switch back.

▶ **Exposure indicator/Exposure Compensation/Rangefinder.** Although Nikon gives this feature a confusing moniker, in simpler terms this is your light meter. When the bars are in the center, you are at the proper settings to get a good exposure; when the bars are to the left, you are underexposed; and when the bars are to the right, you are overexposing your image. This feature is shown when using Manual exposure. When the Exposure Compensation button is set, this display is also shown indicating how much over- or underexposure is being set. When the Rangefinder option is turned on (you can find this in the Setup menu under Viewfinder options) and the lens is set to Manual focus, this shows you a bar graph that indicates distance. When the subject is in focus, the bars are even on both sides of a 0. When the bars are displayed to the left, this indicates that you are focused in front of the subject; bars to the right indicate that the focus is falling behind the subject. Use the focus ring to adjust the focus. The Rangefinder display is not available when shooting in Manual exposure mode.

▶ **FEC indicator.** When this is displayed, your Flash Exposure Compensation is on. Flash Exposure Compensation is used to add or subtract light output from your flash. This applies to both the built-in flash and an accessory Speedlight.

▶ **Exposure compensation indicator.** When this appears in the viewfinder, your camera has exposure compensation activated, and you may not get a correct exposure. Exposure compensation is used to add or subtract from the overall exposure chosen by the camera meter.

▶ **Auto ISO indicator.** This is displayed when the Automatic ISO setting is activated to let you know that the camera is controlling the ISO settings.

▶ **Warning indicator.** When this question mark icon is flashing, the camera is warning you that there may be a problem with your settings. Press the Help button to view the warning.

Information Display

The Information Display, which I will refer to as the Info display for brevity, shows some of the same shooting information that appears in the viewfinder, but there are also quite a few settings that are only displayed here. When this is displayed on the LCD, you can view and change the settings without looking through the viewfinder. When the camera is turned on, the Shooting info is automatically displayed on the LCD monitor. The info remains on display until no buttons have been pushed for about 8 seconds (default) or the Shutter Release button is pressed. You can change the length of time this is displayed in the Setup menu under the Auto-off timers option Playback/menus.

This display shows you everything you need to know about your camera settings. Additionally, the camera has a sensor built in that tells it when the camera is being held vertically, and the Info display is shown upright no matter which way you are holding your camera.

The camera also allows you a number of options on how the information is displayed. You can choose between Classic or Graphic. You can also change the color of the Shooting Info Display. In Classic mode you can choose between black, blue, and orange. In Graphic mode, you can choose between green, black, or brown. You can also choose a different display for the scene and P, S, A, and M modes. These settings can be accessed in the Setup menu under the Info display format heading.

For more info on the Setup menu, see Chapter 3.

▶ **Shooting mode.** This displays the Shooting mode that your camera is currently set to. This can be one of the scene modes, in which case the display will be the appropriate icon, or one of the Semi-auto modes such as P, S, A, or M, in which case the display will show the corresponding letter. This display changes when the Mode dial is rotated.

▶ **Aperture/f-stop number.** This tells you how wide your aperture or lens opening is. The terms *aperture* and *f-stop* are interchangeable. Higher f-numbers denote smaller openings, while lower f-numbers mean that the opening is wider, letting in more light.

▶ **Shutter speed.** This shows in seconds or fractions of seconds how long your shutter stays open when the Shutter Release button is pressed.

▶ **Shutter speed display.** When set to the Graphic mode, this gives you a visual representation about the length of your shutter speed when the camera is held in the horizontal position.

▶ **Aperture display.** When set to Graphic mode, this shows you approximately what your lens opening looks like when the camera is held in the horizontal position.

▶ **Exposure indicator/Rangefinder.** This acts as your light meter. When the bars are in the center, you are at the proper settings to get a good exposure; when the bars are to the left, you are overexposed; when the bars are to the right, you are underexposing your image. This feature is only displayed in Manual exposure. This display blinks when the light is too dark or too bright in P, S, A, or one of the scene modes. It is also displayed when exposure compensation is applied showing how much compensation is applied.

▶ **AF area mode/Selected focus point.** This tells you which AF area mode is selected: Auto-area, Dynamic-area, or Single-point. This also tells you when 3D-tracking is enabled and which focus point is selected when in Single-point AF.

▶ **Help indicator.** When this icon (shown as a question mark) is flashing, there may be a problem with one of your settings. Pressing the Help/Zoom out button will display information on rectifying the problem. When this icon appears and is not flashing, press the Help button to display information on the currently selected option.

▶ **Flash Sync mode.** This shows which mode your flash is set to. You can change the Flash mode by pressing the Flash button and rotating the Command dial. For more information on Flash Sync modes, see Chapter 6.

▶ **Exposure compensation value**. This shows the amount of exposure compensation, if any, that has been set. Exposure compensation is used to increase or decrease the amount of exposure to fine-tune your image.

▶ **Flash Exposure Compensation.** This shows you the amount, if any, of Flash Exposure Compensation (FEC), which is used to make the flash more or less bright. FEC is set by simultaneously pressing the Flash mode button, the Exposure Compensation button, and rotating the Command dial. Rotating to the right decreases flash exposure; rotating to the left increases the exposure.

1.7 LCD display in Wide (landscape) orientation

▶ **Number of remaining exposures.** This shows you approximately how many exposures can be saved to your memory card. When the Preset White Balance is ready to be set, this will blink PRE.

▶ **K.** This icon appears when you have more than 1,000 exposures remaining on your memory card.

▶ **Active D-Lighting indicator.** This shows whether you have Active D-Lighting on or off. Active D-Lighting can be set in the Info display.

▶ **Metering mode.** This displays which metering mode your camera is set to: Matrix, Center-weighted, or Spot. For more information on metering, see Chapter 2.

▶ **AF area mode.** This icon tells you which Autofocus area mode is set. The AF area modes determine how the focus point is chosen.

▶ **Focus mode.** This tells you which focus mode your camera is set to: AF-A (Automatic), AF-C (Continuous), AF-S (Single), or MF (Manual).

▶ **Release mode.** This lets you know what Release mode your camera is set to: Single frame, Continuous, Self-timer, Delayed remote, or Quick response remote.

▶ **ISO sensitivity.** This tells you what your current ISO setting is.

▶ **White balance.** This displays which white balance setting you are currently using.

▶ **Image size.** This tells you the size of the image you are recording.

1.8 LCD display in Tall (portrait) orientation

▶ **Image quality.** This display shows the quality or compression of the JPEG or shows that you are recording a RAW image.

▶ **Battery indicator.** This shows you the remaining charge on your battery.

▶ **Beep indicator.** This icon (musical note) tells you whether you have the camera set to beep when focus is achieved in Single Focus mode. When the icon has a slash through it, the beep is turned off (recommended).

▶ **Picture Control.** This section of the display shows you what Picture Control is being applied to your images. For more information on Picture Controls, see Chapter 3.

▶ **Auto-ISO indicator.** This icon is displayed only when Auto-ISO is enabled.

▶ **Manual flash indicator.** This icon appears when the built-in flash is set to Manual, but only when the flash is popped up. When an optional Speedlight is attached, this icon is displayed when FEC is applied directly on the Speedlight.

▶ **Date imprint indicator.** This icon is shown when the optional date imprint function is applied. This function prints the date at the bottom of the image as it's being recorded.

▶ **Eye-fi indicator.** This icon only appears when using an Eye-fi wireless SD card.

CHAPTER 2

Nikon D3000 Essentials

This chapter covers some of the most commonly changed settings of the camera, such as the exposure modes, metering, AF settings, and ISO. All of these combined settings are used to create your image and can be tweaked and adjusted to reflect your artistic vision or simply to be sure that your pictures come out exactly as you want, even in difficult lighting situations. Also covered in this chapter are discussions about Picture Controls and white balance, both of which affect the colors in your images.

The combination of different camera settings determines how your images look.

Exposure Modes

Exposure modes determine how the different settings are chosen to get the desired exposure. The Nikon D3000 has quite a few options to help you get the exposure that is right for the scene you are photographing.

There are modes that are fully automatic, some that are semiautomatic (in that you choose one aspect of the exposure and the camera takes care of the rest), and a fully manual mode in which you determine all the settings according to your calculations.

Auto modes

The D3000 has two fully automatic, or Auto, modes that do all the work for you. These are simple grab-and-go settings to use when you're in a hurry or you just don't want to be bothered with changing the settings. The Auto modes control everything from shutter speed and aperture to ISO sensitivity and white balance.

The Auto ISO setting can be overridden using the Information Display menu to change the ISO setting. If the Function button is set to ISO, the Auto ISO can be overridden as well. The override remains in effect unless the camera is changed to P, S, A, or M and returned to one of the scene modes. When changing back to a scene mode from P, S, A, or M, the Auto ISO function is again activated.

Auto

The Auto mode is basically a point-and-shoot mode. The camera takes complete control over the exposure. The camera's meter reads the light, the color, and the brightness of the scene and runs the information through a sophisticated algorithm. The camera uses this information to determine what type of scene you are photographing and chooses the settings that it deems appropriate for the scene.

If there isn't enough light to make a proper exposure, the camera's built-in flash pops up when the Shutter Release button is half-pressed for focus. The flash fires when the shutter is released, resulting in a properly exposed image.

This mode is great for taking snapshots, when you simply want to concentrate on capturing the image and let the camera determine the proper settings.

Auto (flash off)

This mode functions in the same way as the Auto setting, except that it disables the flash, even in low-light situations. In instances when the lighting is poor, the camera's

AF-assist illuminator lights up to provide sufficient light to achieve focus. The camera uses the focus area of the closest subject to focus on.

This setting is preferable when you want to use natural or ambient light for your subject or in situations where you aren't allowed to use flash, such as museums, or events where the flash may cause a distraction, such as weddings.

Advanced scene modes

Sometimes the Auto mode isn't going to give you the proper settings to suit your needs, especially when shooting under difficult situations or when you have special circumstances. These scene modes take into account different lighting situations and modify the way the camera meters the light, as well as controlling the focus points, the flash settings, and the aperture, shutter speed, and ISO sensitivity settings.

The camera also determines if there is enough light to make an exposure and activates the built-in flash if there is not enough light. Some of these scene modes, such as Landscape, also make sure that the flash is not used, even in low-light situations.

The scene modes in the D3000 allow you to capture the image with the settings that are best for what you are photographing. The camera has the parameters programmed into it, and you can just rotate the Mode dial to the scene type for the most commonly used scene modes.

These scene modes account for difficult lighting situations and make it easier to get great photos. This can give you a little more flexibility than just sticking the camera in Auto mode and hoping that things turn out as you want them to.

Portrait

This scene mode is for taking pictures of people. The camera automatically adjusts the colors to give natural-looking skin tones. The camera focuses on the closest subject. It also attempts to use a wide aperture, if possible, to reduce the depth of field. This draws attention to the subject of the portrait, leaving distracting background details out of focus.

The built-in flash and AF-assist illuminator automatically activate in low-light situations.

Landscape

This mode is used for taking photos of far-off vistas. The camera automatically adjusts the colors to apply brighter greens and blues to skies and foliage. The camera also automatically focuses on the closest subject and uses a smaller aperture to provide a greater depth of field to ensure focus throughout the entire image.

In this mode, the camera automatically disables the AF-assist illuminator and the flash.

Child

This mode is for taking portraits or candid shots of children. The camera automatically adjusts the colors to give more saturation while still giving a natural skin tone. The camera automatically focuses on the closest subject and uses a fairly small aperture to capture background details. The built-in flash is automatically activated when the light is low.

Sports

This mode uses a fast shutter speed to freeze the action of moving subjects. The camera focuses continuously as long as you have the Shutter Release button half-pressed. The camera also uses predictive focus tracking based on information from all the focus areas in case the main subject moves from the selected focus point.

The camera disables the built-in flash and AF-assist illuminator when this mode is selected.

Close Up

This scene mode is used for close-up or macro shots. It uses a fairly wide aperture to provide a soft background while giving the main subject a sharp focus. In this mode, the camera focuses on the subject in the center of the frame, although you can use the multi-selector to choose one of the other focus points to create an off-center composition.

When light is low, the camera automatically activates the built-in flash. Be sure to remove your lens hood when using the flash on close-up subjects because the lens hood can cast a shadow on your subject by blocking the light from the flash.

Night Portrait

This mode is for taking portraits in low-light situations. The camera automatically activates the flash and uses a longer shutter speed to capture the ambient light from the background. This balances the ambient light and the light from the flash, giving you a more natural effect. I recommend using a tripod when you use this feature to prevent blurring from camera shake that can occur during longer exposure times.

Programmed Auto

Programmed Auto mode (P) is a fully automatic mode suitable for use when shooting snapshots and scenes where you're not very concerned about controlling the settings.

When the camera is in Programmed Auto mode, it decides all the settings for you, based on a set of algorithms. The camera attempts to select a shutter speed that allows you to shoot handheld without suffering from camera shake, while also adjusting your aperture so that you get good depth of field to ensure everything is in focus.

When the camera body is coupled with a lens that has a CPU built in (all autofocus, or AF, lenses have a CPU), the camera automatically knows what focal length and aperture range the lens has. The camera then uses this lens information to decide what the optimal settings should be.

This exposure mode chooses the widest aperture possible until the optimal shutter speed for the specific lens is reached. Then the camera chooses a smaller f-stop and increases the shutter speed as light levels increase.

For example, when using an 18-55mm kit lens, the camera keeps the aperture wide open until the shutter speed reaches about 1/40 second (approximately the minimum shutter speed needed to avoid camera shake). Upon reaching 1/40 second, the camera adjusts the aperture to increase depth of field.

The exposure settings selected by the camera are displayed in both the LCD control panel and the viewfinder display. Although the camera chooses what it thinks are the optimal settings, the camera does not know what your specific needs are. You may decide that your hands are not steady enough to shoot at the shutter speed the camera has selected, or you may want a wider or smaller aperture for selective focus.

Fortunately, you aren't stuck with the camera's exposure choice. You can engage what is known as *flexible program*. Flexible program allows you to deviate from the camera's aperture and shutter speed choice when you are in P mode. This feature can be automatically engaged simply by rotating the Command dial until the desired shutter speed or aperture is achieved. This allows you to choose a wider aperture and faster shutter speed when rotated to the right, or a slower shutter speed and smaller aperture when the dial is rotated to the left.

With flexible program, you can maintain the metered exposure while still maintaining some control over the shutter speed and aperture settings.

A quick example of using flexible program would be if the camera has set the shutter speed at 1/60 second with an aperture of f/8, you're shooting a portrait, and you want a wider aperture to throw the background out of focus. By rotating the Command dial to the right, you can open the aperture up to f/4, which causes the shutter speed to increase to 1/250 second. This is known as an *equivalent exposure,* meaning you get the exact same exposure but the settings are different.

When flexible program is on, an asterisk appears next to the P on the display. Rotate the main Command dial until the asterisk disappears to return to the default Programmed Auto settings.

 When using non-CPU lenses, the camera must be set to Manual exposure **CAUTION** mode.

Aperture Priority

Aperture Priority mode (A) is a semiautomatic mode. In this mode, you decide which aperture to use, and the camera sets the shutter speed for the best exposure based on your chosen aperture. Situations where you may want to select the aperture include when you're shooting a portrait and want a large aperture (small f-number) to blur the background, and when you're shooting a landscape and you want a small aperture (large f-number) to ensure the entire scene is in focus.

 In Aperture Priority mode, if there is not enough light to make a proper expo- **NOTE** sure, the camera displays Lo in place of the shutter speed setting. In the same manner, it will also display Hi if there is too much light.

In my opinion, choosing the aperture to control depth of field is one of the most important parts of photography. This allows you to selectively control which areas of your image are in sharp focus and which areas are allowed to blur and by how much. Controlling depth of field enables you to draw the viewer's eye to a specific part of the image, which can make your images more dynamic and interesting to the viewer.

Shutter Priority

Shutter Priority mode (S) is another semiautomatic mode. In this mode, you choose the shutter speed and the camera sets the aperture. This mode is good to use when shooting moving subjects, sports, or action scenes where you need a fast shutter speed to freeze the motion of your subject and prevent blur.

For more information on using shutter speeds in action and sports photography, see Chapter 7.

You can also select a slower shutter speed to *add* motion blur as a creative photographic technique.

 In Shutter Priority mode, if there is not enough light to make a proper exposure, the camera displays Lo in place of the aperture setting. In the same manner, it will also display Hi if there is too much light.

Manual

When in Manual mode (M), both the aperture and shutter speed settings are set by you. You can estimate the exposure, use a handheld light meter, or use the electronic analog exposure display to determine the exposure needed.

Probably the main question that people have about Manual mode is why you would use it when you have these other modes. There are a few reasons why you may want to set the exposure manually:

▶ **To gain complete control over exposure.** The camera typically decides the optimal exposure based on technical algorithms and an internal database of image information. But what the camera decides is optimal is not necessarily what is optimal in your mind.

   You may want to underexpose to make your image dark and moody, or you may want to overexpose a bit to make the colors pop (making colors bright and contrasty). If your camera is set to M, you can choose the settings and place your image in whatever tonal range you want without having to adjust the exposure compensation settings.

▶ **When using studio flash.** The camera's metering system isn't used when using studio strobes or external nondedicated flash units. When using external strobes, a flash meter or manual calculation is necessary to determine the proper exposure. You can use the Manual exposure mode to quickly set the aperture and shutter speed to the proper exposure; just be sure not to set the shutter speed above the rated sync speed of 1/200 second.

▶ **When using non-CPU lenses.** The camera must be set to Manual exposure mode when you use older non-CPU lenses or an error displays and the shutter release locks, rendering the camera unable to take a picture.

Metering Modes

The D3000 has three metering modes that you can choose from to help you get the best exposure for your image: Matrix, Center-weighted, and Spot. You can change the modes in the Information Display menu or in the Shooting menu.

 Metering modes can only be changed when using P, S, A, or M exposure
NOTE modes.

Metering modes decide how the camera's light sensor collects and processes the information used to determine exposure. Each of these modes is useful for different types of lighting situations.

Matrix

The default metering system that the Nikon cameras use, including the D3000, is a proprietary system called 3D Color Matrix II, or Matrix metering for short. The D3000 has a 420-pixel RGB sensor that measures the intensity of the light and the color of a scene and compares that information to information from 30,000 images stored in its database. Then the camera determines the exposure settings based on the findings from the comparison. Simplified, it works like this: You're photographing a portrait outdoors, and the sensor detects that the light in the center of the frame is much dimmer than the edges. The camera takes this information along with the focus distance and compares it to the ones in the database.

The images in the database with similar light and color patterns and subject distance tell the camera that this must be a close-up portrait with flesh tones in the center and sky in the background. From this information, the camera decides to expose primarily for the center of the frame, although the background may be over- or underexposed. The RGB sensor also takes note of the quantity of the colors and uses that information as well.

2.1 The 420-pixel RGB sensor in the D3000

There are a few types of Matrix metering that are used by the D3000; which type is employed is based upon the type of lens that is attached to the camera body.

For more information on lenses and lens specifications, see Chapter 5.

The Matrix metering setting is highly intuitive, and Nikon has been refining it over a number of years, so it works very well for most subjects. I almost always have my camera set to Matrix.

▶ **3D Color Matrix metering II.** As mentioned earlier, this is the default metering system that the camera employs when a G- or D-type lens is attached to the camera. Most lenses made since the early to mid-1990s are these types of lenses. The only difference between the G- and D-type lenses is that there is no aperture ring on a G-type lens. When using this metering method, the camera decides the exposure setting, mostly based on the brightness of the overall scene and the colors of the subject matter; the camera also takes into account the distance from the subject and which focus point is used.

In addition, the camera takes into account the focal length of the lens to further decide which areas of the image are important to getting the proper exposure. For example, when using a wide-angle lens with a faraway subject and a bright area at the top of the image, the camera sets the exposure so that the sky and clouds don't lose detail.

▶ **Color Matrix metering II.** Most AF lenses made from about 1986 to the early to mid-1990s are non-D and G-type CPU lenses. When this type of Matrix metering is being used, the camera uses only brightness, subject color, and focus information to determine the right exposure.

If a non-CPU lens is attached, the camera's meter defaults to Center-weighted metering.

For more information on lenses, see Chapter 5.

Matrix metering is generally suitable for use with most subjects unless you're in a particularly tricky lighting situation such as when the subject is lit from behind (backlit). Due to the large amount of image data in the Matrix metering database, the camera can usually make a fairly accurate assessment about what type of image you are shooting and adjust the exposure accordingly. For example, with an image that has a high amount of contrast and brightness across the top of the frame, the camera usually tries to set an exposure so that the highlights retain detail. Paired with Active D-Lighting, your exposures will have good dynamic range throughout the entire image.

When shooting a series of images where the exposure needs to be consistent, you may want to choose Center-weighted metering because even small changes in the composition can affect the exposure when using Matrix metering.

Center-weighted

When the camera's metering mode is switched to Center-weighted, the meter takes a light reading of the whole scene but bases the exposure settings mostly on the light falling on the center of the scene. The camera determines about 75 percent of the exposure from an 8mm circular pattern in the center of the frame and 25 percent from the edges.

Center-weighted metering is a very useful option. It works great when shooting photos where you know the main subject will be in the middle of the frame. This metering mode is useful when photographing a dark subject against a bright background, or a light subject against a dark background. This mode works especially well for portraits where you want to preserve the background detail while exposing correctly for the subject.

Center-weighted metering can provide you with consistent results without worrying about the fluctuations in exposure settings that can sometimes happen when using Matrix metering.

Spot

In Spot meter mode, the camera does just that: it meters only a spot. This spot is only 3.5mm in diameter and only accounts for 2.5 percent of the entire frame. The spot is linked to the active focus point, which is good, so that you can focus and meter your subject at the same time.

Spot metering is useful when the subject is the only thing in the frame that you want the camera to expose for. For example, when you are photographing a subject on a completely white or black background, you need not be concerned with preserving detail in the background; therefore, exposing just for the subject works out perfectly. One instance where this mode works well is when doing concert photography where the musician or singer is lit by a bright spotlight. You can capture every detail of the subject and just let the shadow areas go black.

Autofocus Modes

The Nikon D3000 has three autofocus (AF) modes: Continuous (AF-C), Single (AF-S), and Auto (AF-A). Each mode is useful for different types of shooting conditions, from sports to still-life photographs. The AF modes can be changed in the Information Display Menu or in the Shooting menu. Most lenses that work with the D3000, such as the kit lens, also have a switch to enable you to toggle from AF to Manual focus.

 Only AF-S lenses will autofocus with the D3000.

Continuous

When the camera is set to Continuous AF (AF-C), as long as the Shutter Release button is halfway pressed, the camera continues to focus. If the subject moves, the camera activates Predictive Focus Tracking. With Predictive Focus Tracking on, the camera tracks the subject to maintain focus and attempts to predict where the subject will be when the Shutter Release button is pressed completely. When in Continuous AF mode, by default, the camera fires when the Shutter Release button is pressed, whether or not the subject is in focus (this is known as *release priority*). This is the AF mode you want to use when shooting sports or any subject that may be moving erratically.

Single

In Single AF (AF-S) mode, the camera focuses when the Shutter Release button is pressed halfway. When the camera achieves focus, the focus locks. The focus remains locked until you release the shutter or the Shutter Release button is no longer pressed. By default, the camera does not fire unless focus has been achieved (this is known as *focus priority*). This is the AF mode to use when shooting portraits, landscapes, or other photos where the subject is relatively static.

Auto

When the camera is set to Auto mode (AF-A), it automatically chooses between AF-C and AF-S, depending on the subject. If the camera determines that your subject is not moving, it sets the focus mode to AF-S. If the camera detects a moving subject, it sets the focus mode to AF-C. If the camera determines that the subject is moving, focus tracking is activated.

Manual

When set to Manual mode, the D3000 AF system is off. Focus is achieved by rotating the focus ring of the lens until the subject appears sharp when looking through the viewfinder. The Manual focus setting can be used when shooting still-life photographs or other nonmoving subjects, when you want total control of the focus, or simply when you are using a non-AF-S lens. Note that the camera shutter will release regardless of whether the scene is in focus.

When using the Manual focus setting, the D3000 offers a bit of assistance in the way of an electronic rangefinder. The electronic rangefinder can be viewed in the viewfinder display where the light meter is normally displayed.

 For more information on the electronic rangefinder, see Chapter 3.

AF Area Modes

The D3000 has inherited the Multi-CAM 1000 AF module from the professional-level D200 camera. The Multi-CAM 1000 is a very highly regarded and accurate focusing system. It features 11 focus points: one cross-type sensor, eight vertical sensors, and two horizontal sensors.

The D3000 has four AF area modes to choose from: Single-point AF, Dynamic-area AF, Auto-area AF, and 3D-tracking. AF area modes can be changed in the Information Display or the Shooting menu.

The D3000 employs 11 separate AF points. The 11 AF points can be used individually in Single-point AF mode, or you can choose one point and have it work in conjunction with the nonactive points when in Dynamic-area AF mode.

When set to 3D-tracking, the camera maintains sharp focus on a moving subject as it crosses the frame. With 3D-tracking, the camera recognizes distance, color, and light information and then uses it to track the subject across the frame.

Single-point AF mode

Single-point AF mode is the easiest mode to use when you're shooting slow-moving or completely still subjects. You can press the Multi-selector up, down, left, or right, to choose one of the AF points. The camera only focuses on the subject if it's in the selected AF area. The selected AF point is displayed in the viewfinder.

Use Single-point AF when focusing on a particular area is critical.

Dynamic-area AF mode

Dynamic-area AF mode also allows you to select the AF point manually, but unlike Single-point AF, the remaining unselected points remain active; this way, if the subject happens to move out of the selected focus area, the camera's highly sophisticated autofocus system can track it throughout the frame.

When you set the focus mode to AF-S (discussed earlier in this chapter), the mode operates exactly the same as if you were using Single-point AF. To take advantage of Dynamic-area AF, the camera must be set to AF-C mode.

3D-tracking mode

This mode has all 11 AF points active. You select the primary AF point, but if the subject moves, the camera uses 3D-tracking to automatically select a new primary AF point. The camera performs 3D-tracking by using distance and color information from the area immediately surrounding the focus point. The camera uses this information to determine what the subject is, and if the subject moves, the camera selects a new focus point. This mode works very well for subjects moving unpredictably; however, you need to be sure that the subject and the background aren't similar in color.

When photographing a subject with a color similar to that of the background, the camera may lock focus on the wrong area, so use this mode carefully. I have problems with this mode, particularly when shooting team sports, where the players generally wear the same color uniforms. This is because the AF system can't accurately track the subjects due to the similar colors.

Auto-area AF

Auto-area AF mode is exactly what it sounds like: The camera automatically determines the subject and then chooses one or more AF points to lock focus.

Normally, I tend not to use a fully automatic setting such as this, but I've found that it works reasonably well and I can recommend using it when you shoot candid photos. When the camera is set to Single AF mode, the active AF points light up in the viewfinder for about 1 second when the camera attains focus; when in Continuous AF mode, no AF points appear in the viewfinder.

ISO Sensitivity

ISO, which stands for International Organization for Standardization, is the rating for the speed of film, or in digital terms, the sensitivity of the sensor. The ISO numbers are standardized, which allows you to be sure that when you shoot at ISO 100 you get the same exposure no matter what camera you use.

The ISO for your camera determines how sensitive the image sensor is to the light that is reaching it through the lens opening. Increasing or reducing the ISO affects the exposure by allowing you to use faster shutter speeds or smaller apertures (raising the ISO), or using a slower shutter speed or wider aperture (lowering the ISO).

The D3000 has an ISO range from 100 to 1600. In addition to these standard ISO settings, the D3000 also allows you to extend the range of the ISO setting by offering a setting called Hi 1, which is equivalent to an ISO of 3200. You can set the ISO on the D3000 by using the Information display, or by going into the Shooting menu and choosing the ISO sensitivity settings option. The ISO can only be set in 1-stop increments

 Using the Hi 1 setting does not produce optimal results. Using the Hi 1 setting can cause your images to have a high amount of noise.

Auto ISO

The D3000 also offers a feature where the camera adjusts the ISO automatically for you when there isn't enough light to make a proper exposure. Auto ISO is meant to free you up from making decisions about when to raise the ISO. The Auto ISO can be set in the Shooting menu under the ISO sensitivity settings option.

You can limit how high the ISO can be set so that you can keep control of the noise created when a higher ISO is used.

If you manually set the ISO to 400, the Auto ISO function does not allow the ISO to go lower than ISO 400, no matter how bright the scene is. So when using the Auto ISO feature, be sure to set your ISO to 100 to ensure that you can get the full range of ISO settings.

Using Auto ISO can sometimes yield questionable results because you can't be sure what ISO adjustments the camera will make. So if you're going to use it, be sure to set it to conditions that you deem acceptable to ensure that your images will be neither blurry nor noisy.

In the past, I always eschewed using Auto ISO, but because the high ISO perfor-mance on Nikon's newest cameras is pretty good, I have started using it frequently. It especially comes in handy when shooting concerts. This allows me to have a high ISO setting when the lighting is dim, but also reduces the ISO when the lights are turned up on the performer. This setting has actually been quite helpful, allowing me to get many more usable concert photos than I did in the past when I cranked up the ISO and left it set high.

Be sure to set the following options in the Shooting menu/ISO sensitivity settings:

▶ **Maximum sensitivity.** Choose an ISO setting that allows you to get an accept-able amount of noise in your image. If you're not concerned about noisy images, then you can set it all the way up to Hi 1. If you need your images to have less noise, you can choose a lower ISO; the choices are 200, 400, 800, 1600, and Hi 1.

▶ **Minimum shutter speed.** This setting determines when the camera adjusts the ISO to a higher level. At the default, the camera bumps up the ISO when the shutter speed falls to 1/30 second. If you're using a longer lens or you're photo-graphing moving subjects, you may need a faster shutter speed. In that case, you can set the minimum shutter speed up to 1/250 second. On the other hand, if you're not concerned about camera shake, or if you're using a tripod, you can set a shutter speed as slow as 1 second.

The minimum shutter speed is only taken into account when using Programmed Auto or Shutter Priority modes.

Noise reduction

Since the inception of digital cameras, they've been plagued with what is known as noise. Noise, simply put, is randomly colored dots that appear in your image. This is basically caused by extraneous electrons that are produced when your image is being recorded. When light strikes the image sensor in your D3000, electrons are produced. These electrons create an analog signal that is converted into a digital image by the analog-to-digital (A/D) converter in your camera.

There are two specific causes of noise. The first is heat–generated, or *thermal*, noise. While the shutter is open and your camera is recording an image, the sensor starts to generate a small amount of heat. This heat can free electrons from the sensor, which in turn contaminates the electrons that have been created as a result of the light strik-ing the photocells on your sensor. This contamination shows up as noise.

The second cause of digital noise is known as *high ISO noise.* In any type of electronic device, there is background electrical noise. For the most part, it's very miniscule and you never notice it. Cranking up the ISO amplifies the signals your sensor is receiving. Unfortunately, as these signals are amplified, so is the background electrical noise. The higher your ISO, the more the background noise is amplified until it shows up as randomly colored specks.

Digital noise is composed of two elements: *chrominance* and *luminance.* Chrominance refers to the colored specks, and luminance refers mainly to the size and shape of the noise.

Fortunately, with every new camera released, the technology gets better and better, and the D3000 is no excep-

2.2 An example of noise

tion. The D3000 has one of the lowest signal-to-noise ratios of any camera on the market; thus, you can shoot at ISO 1600 and not worry about excessive noise. In some of the older dSLR cameras, shooting at ISO 1600 produced a very noisy image that was not suitable for large prints.

Although the D3000 is very low in noise, there is noise there, especially when shooting above ISO 800 or when using long exposure times. For this reason, most camera manufacturers have built-in noise reduction (NR) features. The D3000 has two types of NR: Long exposure NR and High ISO NR. Each one approaches the noise differently to help reduce it.

 Although the D3000 employs two different types of NR, they are both controlled by one setting simply designated Noise Reduction. Noise Reduction can be turned on or off in the Shooting menu.

Long exposure NR

For any exposure from 10 seconds or longer the camera runs a noise-reduction algorithm. Basically, how this works is that the camera takes a second exposure, this time with the shutter closed, and compares the noise from this dark frame image to the original one. The camera then applies the NR. The noise reduction takes about the same amount of time to process as the length of the shutter speed; therefore, expect to double the time it takes to make one exposure. While the camera is applying NR, the viewfinder displays a message that says "Job nr." No additional images can be taken until this process is finished. If the camera is switched off before the NR is finished, no noise reduction is applied. While the camera is processing, the memory card access lamp is lit and no other functions can be performed.

High ISO NR

When this option is turned on, any image shot at ISO 800 or higher is run through the noise-reduction algorithm. This feature works by reducing the coloring in the chrominance of the noise and combining that with a bit of softening of the image to reduce the luminance noise.

When shooting in RAW format, no actual noise reduction is applied to the image.

For the most part, I choose not to use in-camera NR features. In my opinion, the camera is very aggressive in the NR, and for that reason, there is a loss of detail. For most people, this is a minor quibble and not very noticeable, but for me, I'd rather keep all the available detail in my images and apply noise reduction in post-processing. This way, I can decide for myself how much to reduce the chrominance and luminance rather than letting the camera do it. The camera doesn't know whether you're going to print the image at a large size or just display it on-screen. I say it's better to be safe than sorry.

Noise reduction can be applied in Capture NX2 or by using Adobe Photoshop Camera Raw or some other image-editing software.

White Balance

Light, whether it is sunlight, from an incandescent light bulb, fluorescent, or from a flash, all has its own specific color. This color is measured using the Kelvin scale. This measurement is also known as *color temperature*. The white balance allows you to adjust the camera so that your images look natural no matter what the light source. Because white is the color that is most dramatically affected by the color temperature of the light source, this is what you base your settings on; hence the term *white balance*. The white balance can be changed in the Shooting menu or by pressing the WB button on the top of the camera and rotating the Main Command dial.

The term *color temperature* may sound strange to you. "How can a color have a temperature?" you might ask. Once you understand the Kelvin scale, things make a little more sense.

What is Kelvin?

Kelvin is a temperature scale, normally used in the fields of physics and astronomy, where absolute zero (0 K) denotes the absence of all heat energy. The concept is based on a mythical object called a *black body radiator.* Theoretically, as this black body radiator is heated, it starts to glow. As it is heated to a certain temperature, it glows a specific color. It is akin to heating a bar of iron with a torch. As the iron gets hotter, it turns red, then yellow, and then eventually white before it reaches its melting point (although the theoretical black body does not have a melting point).

The concept of Kelvin and color temperature is tricky as it is the opposite of what you likely think of as "warm" and "cool" colors. For example, on the Kelvin scale, red is the lowest temperature, increasing through orange, yellow, white, and to shades of blue, which are the highest temperatures. Humans tend to perceive reds, oranges, and yellows as warmer and white and bluish colors to be cold. However, physically speaking, the opposite is true as defined by the Kelvin scale.

White balance settings

Now that you know a little about the Kelvin scale, you can begin to explore the white balance settings. The reason that white balance is so important is to ensure that your images have a natural look. When dealing with different lighting sources, the color temperature of the source can have a drastic effect on the coloring of the subject.

For example, a standard light bulb casts a very yellow light; if the color temperature of the light bulb is not compensated for by introducing a bluish cast, the subject can look overly yellow and not quite right.

In order to adjust for the colorcast of the light source, the camera introduces a colorcast of the complete opposite color. For example, to combat the green color of a fluorescent lamp, the camera introduces a slight magenta cast to neutralize the green.

The D3000 has eight white balance settings:

AUTO **Auto.** This setting is best for most circumstances. The camera takes a reading of the ambient light and makes an automatic adjustment. This setting also works well when using a Nikon CLS-compatible Speedlight because the color temperature is calculated to match the flash output. I actually recommend using this setting as opposed to the Flash WB setting.

PRE **PRE.** This setting allows you to choose a neutral object to measure for the white balance. It's best to choose an object that is either white or light gray. The PRE setting is best used under difficult lighting situations such as when there are two different light sources lighting the scene (mixed lighting). You can also use this setting to choose a WB setting from another photo on the memory card.

Incandescent. Use this setting when the lighting is from a standard household light bulb.

Fluorescent. Use this setting when the lighting is from a fluorescent-type lamp. You can also adjust for different types of fluorescent lamps, including high-pressure sodium and mercury vapor lamps. To make this adjustment, go to the Shooting menu and choose White Balance, then Fluorescent. From there, use the Multi-selector to choose one of the seven types of lamps.

Direct sunlight. Use this setting outdoors in the daylight.

Flash. Use this setting when using the built-in Speedlight, a hot-shoe Speedlight, or external strobes.

Cloudy. Use this setting under overcast skies.

Shade. Use this setting when you are in the shade of a tree or a building, or even under an overhang or a bridge any place where the sun is out but is being blocked.

 One accessory you can use to set your white balance is a gray card, which is included with this book. Simply put the gray card in the scene, and balance off of it. See Appendix C for more details.

Figures 2.3 to 2.9 show the different results of using the white balance settings.

2.3 Auto, 2850 K

2.4 Incandescent, 2850 K

2.5 Fluorescent, 3800 K

2.6 Flash, 5500 K

2.7 Daylight, 5500 K

2.8 Cloudy, 6500 K

2.9 Shade, 7500 K

Picture Controls

With the release of the D3 and the D300, Nikon introduced its Picture Control System. All subsequent cameras including the D3000 have also been equipped with this handy option. This feature allows you to quickly adjust your image settings, including sharpening, contrast, brightness, saturation, and hue based on your shooting needs. This is great for photographers who shoot more than one camera and do batch processing to their images. It allows both cameras to record the images the same, so global image correction can be applied without worrying about differences in color, tone, saturation, and sharpening.

Picture Controls can also be saved to the memory card and imported into Nikon's image-editing software, Capture NX2 or View NX. You can then apply the settings to RAW images or even to images taken with other camera models. These Picture Control files can also be saved to a memory card and shared with other Nikon users, either by importing them into Nikon software or loading them directly to another camera.

Original Picture Controls

Right out of the box, the D3000 comes with six Picture Controls installed.

▶ **SD.** This is the Standard setting. This applies slight sharpening and a small boost of contrast and saturation. This is the recommended setting for most shooting situations.

▶ **NL.** This is the Neutral setting. This setting applies a small amount of sharpening and no other modifications to the image. This setting is preferable if you do extensive post-processing to your images.

▶ **VI.** This is also referred to as the Vivid setting. This setting gives your images a fair amount of sharpening, and the contrast and saturation are greatly boosted, resulting in brightly colored images. This setting is recommended for printing directly from the camera or flash card. Personally, I feel that this mode is a little too saturated and often results in unnatural color tones. This mode is not recommended for portrait situations, as skin tones are not reproduced well.

▶ **MC.** This is the Monochrome setting. As the name implies, this option makes the images monochrome. This doesn't simply mean black and white; you can also simulate photo filters and toned images such as sepia, cyanotype, and more.

▶ **PT.** This is the setting for Portraits. This gives you just a small amount of sharpening, which gives the skin a smoother appearance. The colors are muted just a bit to help achieve realistic skin tones.

▶ **LS.** This is the Landscape setting. Obviously, this setting is for shooting landscapes and natural vistas. The saturation of the blues and greens is boosted.

Custom Picture Controls

All the original Picture Controls can be customized to fit your personal preferences. You can adjust the settings to your liking, giving the images more sharpening and less contrast or choosing from a myriad of other options.

 Although you can adjust the original Picture Controls, you cannot save over them, and so there is no need to worry about losing them.

There are a few different customizations to choose from:

▶ **Quick adjust.** This option is not available with the NL setting. This option exaggerates or de-emphasizes the effect of the Picture Control in use. Quick adjust can be set from ±2.

▶ **Sharpening.** This setting controls the apparent sharpness of your images. You can adjust this setting from 0–9, with 9 being the highest level of sharpness. You can also set this to Auto (A) to allow the camera's imaging processor to decide how much sharpening to apply.

▶ **Contrast.** This setting controls the amount of contrast your images are given. In photos of scenes with high contrast (sunny days), you may want to adjust the contrast down; in low-contrast scenes, you may want to add some contrast by adjusting the settings up. You can set this from ±3 or to A.

▶ **Saturation.** This setting controls how vivid or bright the colors in your images are. You can set this between ±3 or to A. This option is not available in the MC setting.

▶ **Hue.** This setting controls how your colors look. You can choose ±3. Positive numbers make the reds look more orange, the blues look more purple, and the greens look more blue. Choosing a negative number causes the reds to look more purple, the blues to look more green, and the greens to look more yellow. This setting is not available in the MC Picture Control setting. I highly recommend leaving this in the default setting of 0.

▶ **Filter Effects.** This setting is only available when set to MC. The monochrome filters approximate the types of filters traditionally used with black-and-white film. These filters increase contrast and create special effects. The options are

- **Yellow.** This adds a low level of contrast. It causes the sky to appear slightly darker than normal and anything yellow to appear lighter.

- **Orange.** This adds a medium amount of contrast. The sky appears darker, giving greater separation between the clouds. Orange objects appear light gray.

- **Red.** This adds a great amount of contrast, drastically darkening the sky while allowing the clouds to remain white. Red objects appear lighter than normal.

- **Green.** This darkens the sky and lightens any green plant life. This color filter can be used for portraits as it softens skin tones.

▶ **Toning.** This setting adds a color tint to your monochrome (black-and-white) images.

- **B&W.** The Black-and-white option simulates the traditional black-and-white film prints done in a darkroom. The camera records the image in black, white, and shades of gray. This mode is suitable for use when the color of the subject is not important. It can be used for artistic purposes or, as with the Sepia mode, to give your image an antique or vintage look.

- **Sepia.** The Sepia color option duplicates a photographic toning process that is done in a traditional darkroom using silver-based black-and-white prints. You may want to use this option

2.10 Black and white

when trying to convey a feeling of antiquity or nostalgia to your photograph. This option works well with portraits as well as still life and architecture. You can also adjust the saturation of the toning from 1 to 7, with 4 being the default and the middle ground.

NOTE Sepia toning a photographic image requires replacing the silver in the emulsion of the photo paper with a different silver compound, thus changing the color or tone of the photograph. Antique photographs were sometimes treated to this type of toning; therefore, the sepia color option gives the image an antique look. The images have a reddish-brown look to them.

- **Cyanotype.** The Cyanotype is another old photographic printing process. The images taken when in this setting are in shades of cyan. Because cyan is considered to be a cool color, this mode is also referred to as cool. This mode can be used to make very interesting and artistic images. You can also adjust the saturation of the toning from 1 to 7, with 4 being the default setting.

2.11 Sepia   **2.12 Cyanotype**

NOTE Cyanotype is one of the oldest printing processes. When exposed to the light, the chemicals that make up the cyanotype turn a deep blue color. This method was used to create the first blueprints and was later adapted to photography.

2.13 Color toning green

- **Color toning.** You can also choose to add colors to your monochrome images. Although this is similar to Sepia and Cyanotype, this type of toning isn't based on traditional photographic processes. This is simply adding a colorcast to a black-and-white image. There are seven color options you can choose from: red, yellow, green, blue-green, blue, purple-blue, and red-purple. As with Sepia and Cyanotype, you can adjust the saturation of these toning colors.

To customize an original Picture Control, follow these steps:

1. **Go to the Set Picture Control option in the Shooting menu.** Press the Multi-selector right.

2. **Choose the Picture Control you want to adjust.** For small adjustments, choose the NL or SD option. To make larger changes to color and sharpness, choose the VI mode. To make adjustments to monochrome images, choose MC. Press the Multi-selector right.

3. **Press the Multi-selector up or down to highlight the setting you want to adjust (sharpening, contrast, and so on).** When the setting is highlighted, press the Multi-selector left or right to adjust the settings. Repeat this step until you've adjusted the settings to your preferences.

4. **Press the OK button to save the settings.**

When the original Picture Control settings have been altered, an asterisk is displayed with the Picture Control setting (SD*, VI*, and so on).

To restore a Picture Control to default settings, follow these steps:

1. **Go to the Set Picture Control option in the Shooting menu.** Press the Multi-selector right.

2. **Choose the Picture Control you want to reset.** Press the Multi-selector right.

3. **Press the Delete (trashcan) button.** A dialog box asking for confirmation is displayed.

4. **Select Yes and press the OK button to reset the Picture Control.** This brings you back to the adjustment menu. Press the Menu button or tap the shutter release button to exit.

Understanding JPEG Compression

JPEG, which stands for Joint Photographic Experts Group, is a method of compressing photographic files and also the name of the file format that supports this type of compression. The JPEG is the most common type of file used to save images on digital cameras. Due to the small size of the file that is created and the relatively good image quality it produces, JPEG has become the default file format for most digital cameras.

The JPEG compression format came into being because of the immense file sizes that digital images produce. Photographic files contain millions upon millions of separate colors, and each individual color is assigned a number; this causes the files to contain vast amounts of data, therefore making the file size quite large.

In the early days of digital imaging, these huge file sizes made it almost impossible for most people to store any number of images on their computers, which usually had relatively small storage capacities. Less than ten years ago, your standard laptop hard drive was only about 5GB. To efficiently store images, there needed to be some sort of file that could be compressed without losing too much of the image data during reconstruction of the file. Enter the Joint Photographic Experts Group. This group of experts designed what we now affectionately know as the JPEG.

The one problem with JPEG compression is that it is *lossy* compression, meaning that it loses information. For the most part, this loss of information is imperceptible to the human eye. The real problem with JPEGs comes from what is known as *generation loss*. Every time a JPEG is opened and resaved, a small amount of detail is lost. After multiple openings and savings, the quality of the image starts to deteriorate as less and less information is available. Eventually, the image may start to look pixelated or jagged (this is known as a JPEG artifact). Obviously, this can be a problem, but the JPEG would have to be opened and resaved many hundreds of times before you would notice a drop in image quality as long you save at high quality settings.

Image size

When saving a file as a JPEG, the D3000 allows you to choose an image size. Reducing the image size is like reducing the resolution on your camera: It allows you to fit more images on your card. The size you choose depends on what your output is going to be.

If you know you'll be printing your images at a large size, then you definitely want to record large JPEGs. If you're going to print at a smaller size (8x10 or 5x7), you can get away with recording at the Medium or Small setting. Image size is expressed in pixel dimensions. The Large setting records your images at 3872x2592 pixels; this gives you a file that's equivalent to a 10-megapixel image. The Medium setting gives you an image of 2896x1944 pixels, which is in effect the same as a 5.6-megapixel camera. The Small size setting gives you a dimension of 1936x1296 pixels, which gives you about a 2.5-megapixel image.

 Image size can only be changed when using the JPEG file format. RAW files are recorded only at the largest size.

Image quality

For JPEGS, in addition to the size setting, which changes the pixel dimension, you have the Quality setting which lets you decide how much of a compression ratio to apply to your JPEG image. Your choices are Fine, Normal, and Basic. JPEG Fine files are compressed to approximately 1:4, Normal to about 1:8, and Basic to about 1:16.

The more compression is applied to the JPEG, the smaller the file size. This reduced file size comes at a cost, though; highly compressed images can suffer from JPEG artifacts.

NEF or RAW Flexibility

Nikon's RAW files are referred to as NEF in Nikon literature. NEF stands for Nikon Electronic File. RAW files contain all the image data acquired by the camera's sensor. When a JPEG is created, the camera applies different settings to the image such as white balance, sharpness, noise reduction, and so on.

RAW versus JPEG

This issue has caused quite a controversy in the digital imaging world, with some people saying that RAW is the only way to go to have more flexibility in processing images, and others saying that if you get it right in-camera, then you don't need to use RAW images. For what it's worth, both factions are right in their own way.

Choosing between RAW and JPEG basically comes down to the final output, or what you're using the images for. Remember that you don't have to choose one file format and stick with it. You can change the settings to suit your needs as you see fit, or you can even choose to record both RAW and JPEG simultaneously.

Here are some reasons to shoot JPEG files:

▶ **Small file size.** JPEGs are much smaller in size than RAW files; therefore, you can fit many more of them on your SD card and later on your hard drive. If space limitations are a problem, shooting JPEG allows you to get more images in less space.

▶ **Printing straight from the camera.** Some people like to print their images straight from the camera or SD card. RAW files can't be printed without first being converted to JPEGs.

▶ **Continuous shooting.** JPEG files, being smaller than RAW files, don't fill up the camera's buffer as quickly, allowing you longer bursts without the frame rate slowing down.

▶ **Less post-processing.** If you're confident in your ability to get the image exactly as you want it at capture, then you can save yourself time by not having to process the image in a RAW converter and save straight to JPEG.

▶ **Snapshots.** JPEG is a good choice if you're just shooting snapshots of family events or if you only plan to post your images on the Internet.

continued

continued

Here are some reasons to shoot RAW files:

▶ **16-bit images.** When converting the file using a RAW converter such as Adobe Camera Raw (ACR) or Capture NX2, you can save your images with 16-bit color information. (When the information is written to JPEG in-camera, the JPEG is saved as an 8-bit file.) This gives you the option of working with more colors in post-processing. This can be extremely helpful when trying to save an under- or overexposed image.

▶ **White balance.** Although the WB that the camera was set to is tagged in the RAW file, it isn't fixed in the image data. Often, the camera can record a WB that isn't quite correct. This isn't always noticeable by looking at the image on the preview. Changing the WB on a JPEG image can cause posterization and usually doesn't yield the best results. Because you have the RAW image data on hand, changing the WB settings doesn't degrade the image at all.

▶ **Sharpening and saturation.** As with WB, these settings are tagged in the RAW file but not applied to the actual image data. You can add sharpening and saturation (or other options, depending on your software).

When the JPEG is saved, the rest of the unused image data is discarded to help ensure a smaller file size. With a RAW file, this image data is saved so that it can be used more extensively in post-processing. In some ways, the RAW file is like a digital negative, in which the RAW files are used in the same way as a traditional photographic negative; that is, you take the RAW information and process it in order to create your final image.

Although some of the same settings are tagged to the RAW file (WB, sharpening, saturation, and so on), these settings aren't fixed and applied as in the JPEG file; as a result, later on, when you import the RAW file into your favorite RAW converter, you can make changes to these settings with no detrimental effects.

Recording your images in RAW format allows you to be more flexible when post-processing your images and generally gives you more control over the quality of the images.

The D3000 saves its RAW files as compressed NEFs. Similar to JPEG compression, some of the image data is lost when these types of files are compressed. The complex algorithms they use to create these files actually run two compression schemes to the same file.

Because our eyes perceive changes in the darker areas of images more than in the lighter areas, the image data for the shadow areas is compressed using a lossless compression, while the midtones and lighter areas are compressed using a lossy method. This compression scheme has very little impact on the image data and allows you be sure that you retain all of your shadow detail. Compressed RAW files allow the file size to be about 30 to 60 percent less than an uncompressed file.

CHAPTER 3

Exploring the Nikon D3000 Menus

The first few sections of the book cover how to change the main settings of your D3000. In this chapter, I delve in depth into the menu options. Here you can tailor the D3000 options to fit your shooting style or to make adjustments to refine the camera settings to fit different shooting scenarios.

The D3000 has quite a few customizable features to make taking pictures much easier for you. You can assign buttons to different functions that you find yourself using frequently. Using the Recent Settings menu you can access settings that you have changed recently.

The menus are accessed by pressing the Menu button on the back of the camera. Use the Multi-selector to scroll through the toolbar on the left side of the LCD.

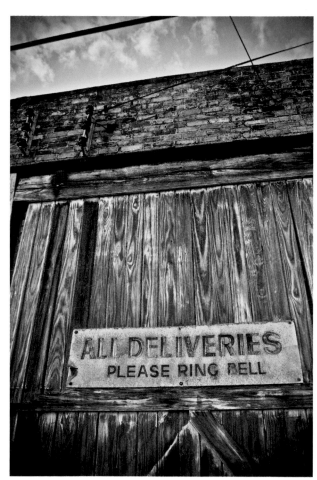

Inside the menus are many different options that let you create dynamic images.

When the desired menu is highlighted in yellow, press the OK button or Multi-selector right to enter the menu. Pressing the Menu button again or tapping the Shutter Release button exits the Menu mode screen and readies the camera for shooting.

When using scene modes, not all menu options are available.

Playback Menu

The Playback menu is where you manage the images stored on the SD card. The Playback menu is also where you control how the images are displayed and what image information is displayed during review. There are eight options available from the Playback menu, which are explained in the following sections. The Playback menu is represented by a Play button icon, similar to the one you would find on a DVD player.

Delete

This option allows you to delete selected images from your memory card or to delete all the images at once.

To delete selected images, choose delete from the Playback menu and follow these steps:

1. **Press the Multi-selector right, highlight Selected (default), and press the Multi-selector to the right again.** The camera displays an image selection screen. You can now select the image you want to delete.

2. **Use the Multi-selector left or right to choose the image.** You can also use the Zoom in button to review the image close up before deleting.

3.1 The Playback menu

3. **Press the thumbnail/Zoom out button to set the image for deletion.** More than one image can be selected. When the image is selected for dele- tion it will show a small trash-can icon in the right-hand corner

4. **Press the OK button to erase the selected images.** The cam- era will ask you for confirmation before deleting the images.

3.2 Selecting images to delete

5. **Select Yes, then press the OK button to delete.** To cancel the deletion, highlight No (default), then press the OK button.

You can also choose to delete all images that were taken on a certain date by follow- ing these steps:

1. **Choose Select date from the Delete options in the Playback menu and then press the Multi-selector right.**

2. **A list of dates is shown along with a thumbnail of one of the images that was taken on that day.** To view all the images taken on that date, press the Thumbnail/Zoom out button. Use the Multi-selector to browse the images. The Zoom in button can be used to take a closer look at any of the images.

3. **Press OK to select the set for deletion.**

4. **Press the Multi-selector right to set or unset the date.** A small box is shown next to the date when a check mark is shown in the box for the images taken on that date that are selected for deletion.

5. **Press the OK button to delete.** A confirmation screen is displayed. Select Yes to delete the images or No to cancel the action.

To delete all images, select Delete from the Playback menu and follow these steps.

1. **Use the Multi-selector to highlight All, and then press the OK button.** The camera will ask you for confirmation before deleting the images.

2. **Select Yes, then press the OK button to delete.** To cancel deletion, highlight No (this is the default setting), then press the OK button.

Protected and hidden images aren't deleted when using the Delete All option. **CAUTION** Protecting and hiding images is covered later in this chapter.

Playback folder

The Nikon D3000 automatically creates folders to store your images in. The main folder that the camera creates is called DCIM; within this folder the camera creates a subfolder to store the images. The first subfolder the camera creates is titled 100D3000. After shooting 999 images the camera automatically creates another folder, 101D3000, and so on. Use this menu to choose which folder or folders to display images from. Keep in mind that if you have used the memory card in another camera and have not formatted it, there will be additional folders on the card (ND200, ND50, and so on).

There are two choices:

- ▶ **Current.** This option displays images only from the folder that the camera is currently saving to. This feature is useful when you have multiple folders from different sessions. Using this setting allows you to preview only the most current images. The current folder can be changed using the Active folder option in the Setup menu.

- ▶ **All.** This option plays back images from all folders that are on the SD card regardless of whether they were created by the D3000.

Display mode

There is quite a bit of image information that is available for you to see when you review images. The Display mode settings allow you to customize the information that is shown when reviewing the images that are stored on your SD card. Enter the Display mode menu by pressing the Multi-selector right. Then use the Multi-selector to highlight the option you want to set. When the option is highlighted press the Multi-selector right or the OK button to set the display feature. The feature is set when a check mark appears in the box to the left of the setting. Be sure to scroll up to Done and press OK to set. If this step is not done the info will not appear in the display.

The Display mode options are

- ▶ **Highlights.** When this option is activated any highlights that are blown out will blink. If this happens you may want to apply some exposure compensation down or reduce your exposure to be sure to capture highlight detail.

▶ **RGB Histogram.** When this option is turned on you can view the separate histograms for the Red, Green, and Blue channels along with a standard luminance histogram.

▶ **Data.** This option allows you to review the shooting data (metering, exposure, lens focal length, and so on).

Generally, the only setting that I use is the RGB Histogram. I can usually tell from the histograms whether the highlights are blown out.

For more information on using histograms, see Chapter 4.

Image review

This option allows you to choose whether the image is shown on the LCD immediately after the image is taken. When this option is turned off, the image can be viewed by pressing the Playback button. Typically, when you take a picture, you want the image to display automatically. This allows you to review the image to check the exposure, framing, and sharpness. There are times, however, when you may not want the images to be displayed. For example, when shooting sports using the continuous release, you may not need to check every shot. Turning this option off also conserves battery power because the LCD is actually the biggest drain on your battery. When in playback mode, the Multi-selector is used to scroll images or change the Info display. I usually turn off the image review when shooting concerts because when the image is being previewed and I press the Multi-selector, the Info display is being changed instead of moving the focus point. Tapping the Shutter Release button cancels the image review, but because I check my images infrequently when shooting concerts, turning it off is much easier for me in the long run.

Rotate tall

The D3000 has a built-in sensor that can tell whether the camera was rotated while the image was taken. This setting rotates images that are shot in portrait orientation to be displayed upright on the LCD screen. I usually turn this option off because the portrait orientation image appears substantially smaller when displayed upright on the LCD.

The options are

▶ **On.** The camera automatically rotates the image to be viewed while holding the camera in the standard upright position.

▶ **Off (default).** When the auto-rotating function is turned off, images taken in portrait orientation are displayed on the LCD sideways in landscape orientation.

I use the Off setting for this option. I prefer to turn the camera and view the image full size. When the image is rotated it is displayed much smaller on the LCD.

Slide show

This allows you to display a slide show of images from the current active folder. You can use this to review the images that you have shot without having to use the Multi-selector. This is also a good way to show friends or clients your images. You can even connect the camera to a TV to view the slide show on a big screen. You can choose an interval of 2, 3, 5, or 10 seconds.

While the slide show is in progress, you can use the Multi-selector to skip forward or backward (left or right), and view shooting info or histograms (up or down). You can also press the Menu button to return to the Playback menu, press the Playback button to end the slide show, or press the Shutter Release button lightly to return to the Shooting mode.

Pressing OK while the slide show is in progress pauses the slide show and offers you the options of restarting the slide show, changing the frame rate, or exiting the slide show. Use the Multi-selector up and down to make your selection then press OK to make your selection.

Print set (DPOF)

DPOF stands for Digital Print Order Format. This option allows you to select images to be printed directly from the camera. This can be used with Pict-bridge-compatible printers or DPOF-compatible devices such as a photo kiosk at your local photo printing shop. This is a pretty handy feature if you don't have a printer at home and want to get some prints made quickly, or if you do have a printer and want to print your photos without downloading them to your computer.

To create a print set:

1. **Use the Multi-selector to choose the Print set (DPOF) option, and then press the Multi-selector right to enter the menu.**

2. **Use the Multi-selector to highlight Select/set, then press the Multi-selector right to view thumbnails.** Press the Zoom in button to view a larger preview of the selected image.

3. **Use the Multi-selector right/left to highlight an image to print.** When the desired image is highlighted, hold the Thumbnail/Zoom out button and press the Multi-selector up or down to set the image and choose the number of prints you want of that specific image. You can choose from 1 to 99. The number of prints and a small printer icon appears on the thumbnail. Continue this procedure until you have selected all the images that you want to print. Press the Multi-selector down to reduce the number of prints and to remove it from the print set.

4. **Press the OK button.** A menu appears with three options:

   • **Done (default).** Press the OK button to save and print the images as they are.

   • **Data imprint.** Press the Multi-selector right to set. A small check mark appears in the box next to the menu option. When this option is set, the shutter speed and aperture setting appear on the print.

   • **Imprint date.** Press the Multi-selector right to set. A small check mark appears in the box next to the menu option. When this option is set, the date the image was taken appears on the print.

5. **If you choose to set the imprint options, be sure to return to the Done option and press the OK button to complete the print set.**

RAW files can't be added to a DPOF print set. If you shoot in RAW you can use the NEF (RAW) processing option in the Retouch menu to create a JPEG copy of the image that can be added to the DPOF print set.

Stop motion movie

This is menu option is where you can quickly find and play any stop motion movies you have created. The Stop motion movie is available as an option in the Retouch menu. For more information on making stop motion movies see Chapter 8.

Shooting Menu

The Shooting menu contains most of the controls that deal with your image settings. This is where you find the most important settings such as ISO, white balance, Active D-Lighting, noise reduction, and others. You also find the settings that deal with auto-focus (AF) and your release modes. A lot of the most commonly changed settings from this menu can also be accessed in the Information Display menu, which is covered later in the chapter. The Shooting menu is represented in the Menu tab by a camera icon.

Reset shooting options

Quite simply, this menu option resets all of the Shooting menu options back to default. Throughout the rest of this section I will note which setting is the default for each option.

Set Picture Control

This is a menu you might find yourself using quite often. Picture Controls allow you to choose how the images are processed and they can also be used in Nikon's image-editing software, Nikon ViewNX and Nikon Capture NX2. These Picture Controls allow you to get the same results when using different cameras that are compatible with the Nikon Picture Control System.

This option is not available when the camera is set to any of the scene modes or the fully automatic modes.

There are six standard Nikon Picture Controls available in the D3000:

3.3 The Shooting menu

▶ **Standard (SD).** This applies slight sharpening and a small boost of contrast and saturation. This is the recommended setting for most shooting situations.

▶ **Portrait (PT).** This setting gives your subject natural color and smooth skin tones.

▶ **Neutral (NL).** This setting applies a small amount of sharpening and no other modifications to the image. This setting is preferable if you often do extensive post-processing to your images.

▶ **Vivid (VI).** This setting gives your images a fair amount of sharpening. The contrast and saturation are boosted dramatically resulting in brightly colored images. This setting is recommended for printing directly from the camera or SD card as well as for shooting landscapes. Personally, I feel that this mode is a little too saturated and often results in unnatural color tones. This mode is not recommended for portrait situations, as skin tones are not reproduced well.

3.4 Picture Control grid

▶ **Monochrome (MC).** As the name implies, this option makes the images monochrome. This doesn't simply mean black and white, but you can also simulate photo filters and toned images such as sepia, cyanotype, and more.

▶ **Landscape (LS).** This Picture Control boosts the saturation of the greens and the blues for vibrant foliage and skies.

All these standard Nikon Picture Controls can be adjusted to suit your specific needs or tastes. In the color modes — SD, PT, NL, VI, and LS — you can adjust the sharpening, contrast, hue, and saturation. In MC mode you can adjust the sharpening, contrast, filter effects, and toning. To adjust the Picture Control simply press the Multi-selector right. This brings up a submenu.

The D3000 also allows you to view a grid graph that shows you how each of the Picture Controls relates to each other in terms of contrast and saturation. Each Picture Control is displayed on the graph represented by a square icon with the letter of the Picture Control it corresponds to. Standard Picture Controls that have been modified are displayed with an asterisk next to the letter. Picture Controls that have been set with one or more auto settings are displayed in green with lines extending from the icon to show you that the settings will change depending on the images.

To view the Picture Control grid select the Picture Control option from the Shooting menu. Press OK and the Picture Control list is displayed. Press the Thumbnail/Zoom out button to view the grid. Once the Picture Control grid is displayed you can use the Multi-selector to scroll though the different Picture Control settings. Once you have highlighted a setting, you can press the Multi-selector right to adjust the settings or press OK to set the Picture Control. Press the Menu button to exit back to the Shooting menu or tap the Shutter Release button to ready the camera for shooting.

 When saving to NEF the Picture Controls are imbedded into the metadata. Only Nikon's software can use these settings. When opening RAW files using a third-party program such as Adobe Camera RAW in Photoshop the Picture Controls are not used.

Image quality

This menu option allows you to change the image quality of the file. You can choose from these options:

▸ **NEF (RAW) + JPEG basic.** This option saves two copies of the same image, one in RAW and one in JPEG with high compression.

▸ **NEF (RAW).** This option saves the images in RAW format.

▸ **JPEG fine.** This option saves the images in JPEG with minimal compression.

▸ **JPEG normal.** This option saves the images in JPEG with standard compression.

▸ **JPEG basic.** This option saves the images in JPEG with high compression.

These settings can also be changed in the Info display.

 For more detailed information on image quality, compression, and file formats, see Chapter 2.

Image size

This allows you to choose the size of the JPEG files. Change the image size depending on the intended output of the file or to save space on your memory card.

The choices are

▸ **Large.** This setting gives you a full resolution image of 3872 × 2592 pixels or 10 megapixels.

▸ **Medium.** This setting gives you a resolution of 2896 × 1944 pixels or 5.6 megapixels.

▸ **Small.** This setting gives your images a resolution of 1936 × 1296 pixels or 2.5 megapixels.

For more detailed information on image size, see Chapter 2

The Image size can also be changed in the Info display.

White balance

You can change the white balance options using this menu option. You can select a WB setting from the standard settings (auto, incandescent, fluorescent, direct sunlight, flash, cloudy, shade) or you can manually set the WB using the PRE setting.

For detailed information on white balance settings and color temperature, see Chapter 2.

Using standard WB settings

To select one of the standard settings, choose the White balance option from the shooting menu, then use the Multi-selector button to highlight the preferred setting, and press the Multi-selector right or the Multi-selector center button. This brings up a new screen that gives you the option to fine-tune the standard setting. Displayed on this screen is a grid that allows you to adjust the color tint of the WB setting selected.

The horizontal axis of the grid allows you to adjust the color from amber to blue making the image warmer or cooler while the vertical axis of the grid allows you to change the tint by adding a magenta or green cast to the image. You can use the Multi-selector to choose a setting from 1 to 6 in either direction; additionally, you can add points along the horizontal and vertical axes simultaneously. For example, you can add 4 points of amber to give it a warmer tone and also add 2 points of green shifting the amber tone more toward yellow.

3.5 The WB fine-tuning grid

Choosing the fluorescent setting brings up some additional menu options; you can choose among seven nonincandescent lighting types. This is handy if you know what specific type of fixture is being used. For example, I was shooting a night football game recently. I had the camera set to Auto WB, but I was getting very different colors from shot to shot and none of them looked right. Because I wasn't shooting RAW I needed to get more consistent shots. I knew that most

3.6 Fluorescent lamp options menu

outdoor sporting arenas used mercury-vapor lights to light the field at night. I selected the fluorescent WB setting from the Shooting menu and chose the #7 option, High temp. Mercury vapor. I took a few shots and noticed I was still getting a sickly green-ish cast so I went back to the fine-tuning option and added 2 points of magenta to cancel out the green colorcast. This gave me an accurate and consistent color.

There are seven settings:

- ▶ **Sodium-vapor.** These are the types of lights often found in streetlights and parking lots. They emit a distinct deep yellow color.

- ▶ **Warm-white fluorescent.** These types of lamps give a white light with a bit of an amber cast to add some warmth to the scene. These lights burn at around 3000K, similar to an incandescent bulb.

- ▶ **White fluorescent.** These lights cast a very neutral white light at around 5200K.

- ▶ **Cool-white fluorescent.** As the name suggests, this type of lamp is a bit cooler than a white fluorescent lamp and has a color temperature of 4200K.

- ▶ **Day white fluorescent.** This lamp approximates sunlight at about 5500K.

- ▶ **Daylight fluorescent.** This type of lamp gives you about the same color as day-light. This lamp burns at about 6300K.

- ▶ **Mercury-vapor.** These lights vary in temperature depending on the manufac-turer and usually run between 4200 and 5200K.

Preset white balance

Preset white balance allows you to make and store up to five custom white balance settings. You can use this option when shooting in mixed lighting; for example, in a room with an incandescent light bulb and sunlight coming in through the window, or when the camera's auto white balance isn't quite getting the correct color.

You can set a custom white balance in two ways: direct measurement, this is when you take reading from a neutral colored object (the gray card included with the book works great for this) under the light source; or copy from existing photograph, this allows you to choose a WB setting directly from an image that is stored on your memory card.

Direct measurement

To take a direct measurement for white balance, follow these steps:

1. **Place a neutral object (preferably a gray card) under the light source you want to balance for.**

2. **Select White balance from the Shooting menu.** Use the Multi-selector to scroll down to Preset manual and press OK. This brings up the White balance preset manual screen.

3. **Select Measure from the menu and press OK.** A dialog box is displayed asking you to confirm that you want to overwrite the existing preset. Select yes and press OK.

4. **Looking through the viewfinder, frame the reference object.** Press the Shutter Release button as if you were taking a photo.

5. **If the camera is successful in recording the white balance, "GD" flashes in the viewfinder control panel and a "data acquired" message is displayed in the info settings on the LCD panel.** If the scene is too dark or too bright, the camera may not be able to set the WB; in this case No Gd flashes in the viewfinder control panel and a message is displayed on the LCD, "Unable to measure preset white balance. Please try again." Tap the Shutter Release button to clear the message, and it's set to take another reading. Adjust the exposure and reshoot.

3.7 The shooting info when presetting WB

When presetting a custom WB, it's usually best to switch the camera to Manual focus because the AF system will have a hard time focusing on an object with little contrast, such as a gray card. You don't need to be in focus to set the WB.

Copy white balance from existing photograph

As I mentioned before, you can also copy the white balance setting from any photo that is saved on the memory card that's inserted into your camera. You can do this if you're shooting in a similar lighting situation or if you simply like the effect.

 If you have particular settings that you like you may consider saving the images on a small memory card. This way you can always have your favorite WB presets saved so you don't accidentally erase them from the camera.

1. **Press the menu button.** Use the Multi-selector to choose White balance from the Shooting menu.

2. **Select Preset manual from the White balance menu.** Press the Multi-selector button right or press OK to view the preset choices.

3. **Use the Multi-selector to highlight Use photo.** You have two options; This image, which is the current image being used for WB reference (either selected from the camera or custom shot), or Select image.

4. **Use the Multi-selector to highlight Select image.** Press OK and the folders on the SD card are displayed. Highlight the appropriate folder and press OK.

5. **The LCD displays thumbnails of the images saved to your SD card.** This is similar to the Delete and DPOF thumbnail display. Use the Multi-selector directional buttons to scroll through the images. You can zoom in on the highlighted image by pressing the Zoom-in button.

6. **Once the desired image is highlighted press OK.** Select this image and press OK to save the setting or choose Select image to choose a different photo.

ISO sensitivity settings

This menu option allows you to set the ISO sensitivity. This is also where you set the parameters for the Auto-ISO feature.

 For more information on ISO settings and Auto ISO, see Chapter 2.

Active D-Lighting

Active D-Lighting is a setting that is designed to help ensure that you retain highlight detail when shooting in a high-contrast situation, such as shooting a picture in direct bright sunlight, which can cause dark shadows and bright highlight areas. Active D-Lighting basically tells your camera to underexpose the image a bit; this underexposure helps keep the highlights from becoming blown out and losing detail. The D3000 also uses a subtle adjustment to avoid losing any detail in the shadow area that the underexposure may cause.

 Active D-Lighting is a separate and different setting than the D-Lighting option CAUTION found in the Retouch menu. For more information on standard D-Lighting, see Chapter 8.

Using Active D-Lighting changes all the Picture Control brightness and contrast settings to Auto; adjusting the brightness and contrast is how Active D-Lighting keeps detail in the shadow areas.

When using Active D-Lighting some extra time is required to process the images. Because your buffer fills up more quickly when shooting continuously, expect shorter burst rates.

Color space

Color space simply describes the range of colors — also known as the gamut — that a device can reproduce. You have two choices of color spaces with the D3000: sRGB and Adobe RGB. The color space you choose depends on what the final output of your images will be.

▶ **sRGB.** This is a narrow color space, meaning that it deals with fewer colors than the larger Adobe RGB color space. The sRGB color space is designed to mimic the colors that can be reproduced on most low-end monitors and is more saturated than the Adobe RGB color space.

▶ **Adobe RGB.** This color space has a much broader color spectrum than is available with sRGB. The Adobe gamut was designed for dealing with the color spectrum that can be reproduced with most high-end printing equipment.

This leads to the question of which color space you should use. As I mentioned earlier, the color space you use depends on what the final output of your images is going to be. If you take pictures, download them straight to your computer, and typically only view them on your monitor or upload them for viewing on the Web, then sRGB will be fine. The sRGB color space is also useful when printing directly from the camera or memory card with no post-processing.

If you are going to have your photos printed professionally or you intend to do a bit of post-processing to your images, using the Adobe RGB color space is recommended. This allows you to have subtler control over the colors than is possible using a narrower color space like sRGB.

For the most part, I capture my images using the Adobe RGB color space. I then do my post-processing and make a decision on the output. Anything that I know I will be posting to the Web I convert to sRGB; anything destined for my printer is saved as Adobe RGB. I usually end up with two identical images saved with two different color spaces. Because most Web browsers don't recognize the Adobe RGB color space, any images saved as Adobe RGB and posted on the Internet will usually appear dull.

Noise reduction

Quite simply this is where you turn on the Noise Reduction function. Noise reduction is covered in depth in Chapter 2.

Release mode

The release mode controls how the shutter release functions. There are a number of different options.

▶ **Single frame.** This is the simplest release mode. One press of the Shutter Release button shoots off one frame. To shoot another frame the button must be completely released and pressed again. Even if the Shutter Release button is held down the camera only releases the shutter once. This is the setting to use for shots of most subjects.

▶ **Continuous release.** In this mode the camera fires the shutter repeatedly as long as the shutter button is pressed and held down. The camera will fire at 3 frames per second (fps) until the buffer fills up, at which point the frame rate slows down. How long it takes for the buffer to fill up is dependent on the SD card you are using. Faster-rated cards allow the buffer to empty out more quickly as the data can be written from the buffer to the card at a higher rate. This means you can shoot at 3 fps for a longer period of time. To be perfectly honest, I used a SanDisk Extreme III SD card, which is one of the fastest on the market, and I have trouble getting the D3000 to sustain 3 fps for longer than 2 seconds when shooting RAW. Sometimes I find the camera bogging down after only 2 shots. Bottom line: The D3000 isn't a speed demon so don't expect to fire off any rapid sports sequences with it, but it works for simple things such as catching the fleeting expressions of a child.

 To be sure you are getting the fastest continuous shooting speed, make sure that your shutter speed is at least 1/125 second and Active D-Lighting is off, and set your Image Quality to a JPEG setting.

▶ **Self-timer.** This setting releases the shutter after a predetermined amount of time when the Shutter Release button is pressed. The default time is 10 seconds, but the time can be adjusted in the Setup menu (Self-Timer Delay). This feature is handy for doing self-portraits, for hopping into a group picture, or for reducing vibration when doing long exposure with the camera on a tripod (the delay of the self-timer allows the camera to steady after pressing the Shutter Release button).

The next two release mode options require an optional ML-L3 wireless remote control. This is a great little accessory that you can usually get for less than $20 and is worth every penny. Similar to the self-timer the remote is great for doing self-portraits, for getting yourself into a group picture, or for reducing vibration when doing long exposures with the camera on a tripod.

▶ **Delayed remote.** This setting releases the shutter after a 2-second delay once the ML-L3 button is pressed.

▶ **Quick-response remote.** This setting releases the shutter as soon as the ML-L3 button is pressed.

Focus mode

This menu option allows you to change the focus mode. You can choose from Auto (AF-A), Single (AF-S), Continuous (AF-C), or Manual focus. Focus modes are covered in depth in Chapter 2. This option can also be changed in the Info display.

AF-area mode

This option is used to select the AF area mode, which controls how the focus point is selected. The AF area modes are also covered in more detail in Chapter 2.

 If the lens is switched to Manual focus the Focus mode and AF-area mode options are "grayed out" and unavailable in the menu

AF-assist

The AF-assist illuminator lights up when there isn't enough light for the camera to focus properly. The camera needs a certain amount of light for the AF to detect contrast in the subject.

In certain instances, even in low light, you may want to turn this option off, such as when shooting faraway subjects in dim settings (concerts or plays). When set to On, the AF-assist illuminator lights up in a low-light situation only when in AF-S mode and Auto-area AF is chosen. When in Single-point mode or Dynamic-area AF is chosen, the center AF point must be active.

When set to Off, the AF-assist illuminator does not light at all even in dim lighting.

Metering

This option is used to select the type of exposure metering the camera uses to determine exposure. The choices are Matrix, Center-weighted, and Spot. Metering modes are covered in depth in Chapter 2.

Built-in flash

This option is used to set how the built-in flash determines the exposure. You can set it to TTL (default), which is the recommended setting or you can choose to set the exposure manually (M). When Manual is selected a submenu is displayed that allows you to choose from six settings: Full, 1/2, 1/4, 1/8, 1/16, or 1/32.

 For more information on using flash and determining flash settings manually, see Chapter 6.

Setup Menu

The Setup menu contains options that don't get changed very much but a lot of them are pretty important. The settings control different things from the brightness of the LCD to controlling what function different buttons are assigned to.

Reset setup options

This option, as with the similar option in the Shooting Menu, allows you to reset all the Setup menu options back to the default settings.

Format memory card

Formatting your card is a much more thorough way of erasing the images on your SD card. Formatting the card redefines the file directory of the card. Deleting images one by one or deleting all images at once leaves blank spaces on the card where image data is filled in as it is being captured. This can cause your image data to become fragmented; although this fragmentation doesn't necessarily cause problems, as the data becomes more and more fragmented the likelihood of your data being corrupted gets greater. Formatting the SD card allows the data to be written in a more organized way. Bottom line is that formatting the SD card should be done every time you are finished downloading your images.

LCD brightness

This menu sets the brightness of your LCD screen. You may want to make it brighter when viewing images in bright sunlight or make it dimmer when viewing images indoors or to save battery power. You can adjust the LCD ±3 levels. The menu shows a graph with ten bars from black to gray and on to white. The optimal setting is where you can see a distinct change in color tone in each of the bars. If the last two bars on the right blend together your LCD is too bright; if the last two bars on the left side blend together your LCD is too dark.

3.8 The Setup menu

Info display format

This menu option is how you set the different display options for the LCD shooting information. You can choose between displaying the shooting information in the Classic format or the Graphic format in three colors. The Graphic format allows you to see a visual representation of the shutter speed and aperture to give you a better idea of what the settings are. Additionally you can also choose for the camera to display the shooting information differently depending on whether you're using the auto and scene modes or the P, S, A, or M modes.

3.9 The Classic shooting information

Auto info display

Setting this to On (default) brings up the Info display when the Shutter Release button is half-pressed and released. When the camera is auto-focusing the display is turned off. The

3.10 The Graphic shooting information

settings are set individually for P, S, A, and M modes and the Auto and scene modes. I prefer to keep mine turned off and press the Info button to display the screen if I need to see it.

Clean image sensor

This is a great feature that was released with the D300 and filtered down to the D3000. The camera uses ultrasonic vibration to knock any dust off the filter in front of the sensor. This helps keep some of the dust off of your sensor but is not going to keep it absolutely dust free forever. You may have to have the sensor professionally cleaned periodically.

You can choose Clean now, which cleans the image sensor immediately, or you have four separate options for cleaning, which you access in the Clean at startup/shutdown option. These include:

▶ **Startup.** The camera goes through the cleaning process immediately upon turning the camera on. This may delay your startup time a little bit.

▶ **Shutdown.** The camera goes through the cleaning process immediately upon turning the camera off.

▶ **Startup and shutdown.** The camera cleans the image sensor when the camera is turned on and also when it is powered down.

▶ **Cleaning off.** This disables the sensor cleaning feature unless activated manually.

Mirror Lock-up

This locks up the mirror to allow access to the image sensor for inspection or for additional cleaning. The sensor is also powered down to reduce any static charge that may attract dust. Because it's a fairly simple process, some people prefer to clean their own sensor; however, especially for beginners, I recommend taking your camera to an authorized Nikon service center for any sensor cleaning. Any damage caused to the sensor by improper cleaning is NOT covered by warranty and can lead to a very expensive repair bill.

Video mode

There are two options in this menu: NTSC and PAL. Without getting into too many specifics, these are types of standards for the resolution of televisions. All of North America, including Canada and Mexico, uses the NTSC standard, while most of Europe and Asia use the PAL standard. Check your television owner's manual for the specific setting if you plan to view your images on a TV directly from the camera.

Time zone and date

This is where you set the camera's internal clock. You also select a time zone, choose the date display options, and turn the daylight-saving time options on or off.

Start by setting the time zone. The display shows a map and a list of cities in the time zone in case you are traveling and unsure of which time zone you're in. Next, set the date and time using the Multi-selector left or right to scroll between the options (year, month, date, hour, minute, and seconds). Use the Multi-selector up or down to change the settings. Press OK when finished.

You can also change the format in which the date is displayed. The choices are Y/M/D, M/D/Y, or D/M/Y.

For places that observe daylight saving time, there is an option to turn this on or off.

Language

This is where you set the language that the menus and dialog boxes display. English is the default language. If you accidentally change it, don't worry; English is marked clearly in English no matter what language is selected.

Image comment

You can use this feature to attach a comment to the images taken by your D3000. You can enter the text using the Input Comment menu. The comments can be viewed in Nikon's Capture NX2 or ViewNX software or can be viewed in the photo info on the camera. Setting the Attach comment option applies the comment to all images taken until this setting is disabled. Some comments you may want to attach are copyright information or your name, or even the location where the photos were taken.

Auto image rotation

This tells the camera to record the orientation of the camera when the photo is shot (portrait or landscape). This allows the camera and also image-editing software to show the photo in the proper orientation so you don't have to take the time in post-processing to rotate images shot in portrait orientation.

Dust Off ref photo

This option allows you to take a dust reference photo that shows any dust or debris that may be stuck to your sensor. Nikon Capture NX2 then uses the image to automatically retouch any subsequent photos where the specks appear. If you have a dusty sensor, this can save you a lot of time by having the retouching automatically applied for you.

To use this feature, either select Start or Clean sensor and then start. Next, you are instructed by a dialog box to take a photo of a bright featureless white object that is about 10 cm from the lens. The camera automatically sets the focus to infinity. A dust off reference photo can only be taken when using a CPU lens. It's recommended to use at least a 50mm lens, and when using a zoom lens you should zoom all the way in to the longest focal length.

Auto off timers

These four menu options are used to determine how long the camera's exposure meter and LCD monitor are active before turning off when no other actions are being performed. They include:

▶ **Short.** When this option is selected, the menus and playback turn off after 8 seconds, the image review after 4 seconds, and the meter shuts off after 4 seconds.

▶ **Normal.** When this option is selected, the menus and playback turn off after 12 seconds, the image review after 4 seconds, and the meter shuts off after 8 seconds.

▶ **Long.** When this option is selected, the menus and playback turn off after 20 seconds, the image review after 20 seconds, and the meter shuts off after 60 seconds.

▶ **Custom.** You can use this option to customize the auto off timer for each operation, Playback/menus, Image review, and Auto meter-off. The options for each are as follows:

  • **Playback/menus.** 8 sec, 12 sec, 20 sec, 1 min, or 10 min

  • **Image review.** 4 sec, 8 sec, 20 sec, 1 min, or 10 min

  • **Auto meter-off.** 4 sec, 8 sec, 20 sec, 1 min, or 30 min

Self-timer delay

This is where you set the delay time for the self-timer. As discussed earlier, the self-timer is handy for when you want to do a self-portrait and you need some time to get yourself into the frame. The self-timer can also be employed to reduce camera shake caused by pressing the Shutter Release button on long exposures. You can set this at 2, 5, 10, or 20 seconds.

Remote on duration

This setting controls how long the camera waits for a signal from the optional ML-L3 infrared remote control before the camera exits the Remote release mode and returns to the default release mode (Single frame). The choices are 1, 5, 10, or 15 minutes.

Beep

When this option is on, the camera emits a beep when the self-timer is counting down or when the AF locks in Single focus mode. You can choose On or Off. For most photographers, this option is absolutely the first thing that gets turned off when the camera is taken out of the box. Although the beep can be kind of useful when in Self-timer mode, it's a pretty annoying option especially if you are photographing in a relatively quiet area.

Viewfinder options

There are a couple of options in the menu to help you with shooting, the viewfinder grid and the rangefinder. When the viewfinder grid option is turned on, there is a grid displayed in the viewfinder to help you with composition. The default setting is off, but personally I like having the grid there to remind me to keep things straight.

When the Rangefinder option is turned on and the lens is set to Manual focus, this shows you a bar graph that indicates distance. When the subject is in focus, the bars are even on both sides of a 0. When the bars are displayed to the left, this indicates that you are focused in front of the subject; bars to the right indicate that the focus is falling behind the subject. Use the focus ring to adjust the focus. The Rangefinder display is not available when shooting in Manual exposure mode. This is a handy feature when using a Manual focus lens or an older non-AF-S lens that doesn't autofocus with the D3000.

File number sequence

The D3000 names files by sequentially numbering them. This option controls how the sequence is handled. When set to Off, the file numbers reset to 0001 when a new folder is created, a new memory card is inserted, or the existing memory card is formatted. When set to On, the camera continues to count up from the last number until the file number reaches 9999. The camera then returns to 0001 and counts up from there. When this is set to Reset, the camera starts at 0001 when the current folder is empty. If the current folder contains images, the camera starts at one number higher than the last image in the folder.

Buttons

This option allows you to customize a few different buttons so that you can quickly change settings depending on your preferences. There are three options.

▶ **Self-timer/Fn. button.** This button can be assigned a number of functions.

  ● **Self-timer.** This is the default setting. Pressing it once turns on the Self-timer; pressing it again switches back to the release mode that was previously set. Once the shutter is released, the release mode is switched back to the previous setting.

  ● **Release mode.** Pressing the button and rotating the Command dial changes the release mode.

- **Image quality/size.** Pressing the button and rotating the Command dial changes the image quality and size.

- **ISO sensitivity.** Pressing the button and rotating the Command dial changes the ISO sensitivity.

- **White balance.** Pressing the button and rotating the Command dial adjusts the white balance settings.

- **Active D-Lighting.** Pressing the button and rotating the Command dial turns Active D-Lighting on or off.

- **Set framing grid.** Pressing the button and rotating the Command dial turns the grid in the viewfinder on and off.

▶ **AE/AF Lock.** You can set this button to different types of settings that all relate to autoexposure or autofocus. The choices are: AE/AF Lock, AE Lock only, AF Lock only, AE Lock (hold), or AF-ON. AE Lock (hold) locks the exposure; one press of the button locks the exposure until the button is pressed again or the shutter is released. AF-ON engages the AF in the same way that half-pressing the Shutter Release button does.

▶ **AE Lock.** This setting allows you the option of locking the exposure when the Shutter Release button is half-pressed. This allows you to focus and take a meter reading of the subject and then recompose the shot without losing the proper exposure for the subject.

No memory card

By default, when no memory card is inserted into the camera, the shutter release is disabled. You can use this option to allow the shutter to release. The options are

▶ **LOCK.** This locks the shutter, not allowing the camera to fire.

▶ **OK.** This enables the shutter to be released when no SD card is in the camera.

Date imprint

Turning this option on imprints your images with the date and/or time that they were shot. You can choose to imprint only the date, the time and date, or the date counter, which displays the number of days that have elapsed between the date that the picture was taken and a selected date.

Once the date is imprinted, it cannot be removed except by cropping.

Active folder

As discussed earlier, the D3000 automatically creates folders in which to store your images. The camera creates a folder named DCIM then stores the images in subfolders starting with folder 100D3000. When the folder gets 999 images in it, the camera automatically starts a new folder. You can choose to rename this folder or change the folder that the camera is saving to. You can name this folder whatever you like (as long as it's no longer than four characters). You can use this option to separate subjects into different folders. When I shoot SCCA sports car races, there are different groups of cars. I use a different folder for each group to make it easier to sort through the images later. If there are five groups, I start out naming my folder GRP1, then GRP2 for the second group, and so on. If you are on a road trip, you can save your images from each destination to separate folders. These are just a couple of different examples of how this feature can be used.

When selecting the active folder, you can choose a new folder or you can select a folder that has already been created. When you format your SD card, all preexisting folders are deleted and the camera creates a folder with whatever number the active folder is set to. So if you set it to a folder named ABC01, when the card is formatted the camera will create folder 100ABC01.

Firmware version

This menu option displays which firmware version your camera is currently operating under. Firmware is a computer program that is embedded in the camera that tells it how to function. Camera manufacturers routinely update the firmware to correct for any bugs or to make improvements on the camera's functions. Nikon posts firmware updates on its Web site at www.nikonusa.com.

Retouch Menu

The Retouch menu allows you to make changes and corrections to your images with the use of imaging-editing software. As a matter of fact, you don't even need to download your images. You can make all the changes in-camera using the LCD preview (or hooked up to a TV if you prefer).

The options include D-Lighting, Red-eye correction, Trim, Monochrome, Color effects, Color balance, and Image overlay.

 The Retouch Menu is discussed at length in Chapter 8.

CHAPTER 4

Essential Photography Concepts

This chapter may contain some photography concepts that are very familiar to some users of this camera and completely new to those who may be new to dSLRs or to photography in general. Even if you're an advanced user, you may find some important information on evaluating your exposure, using histograms, and adjusting your exposure using the exposure compensation and bracketing features of the Nikon D3000. This chapter covers information on exposure, the effects aperture has on depth of field, how the shutter speed is used to create different effects, and how ISO can affect both your aperture and shutter speed settings.

Understanding photographic concepts like how aperture and distance relate to depth of field allows you to add creative elements to your images.

Understanding Exposure

Exposure is the most important aspect of photography. If you don't understand how exposure is calculated you're going to have problems understanding how your camera chooses the settings when using one of the semiautomatic modes like Shutter Priority or Aperture Priority. This can hinder your ability to achieve a specific effect in your image.

By definition, *exposure* as it relates to digital photography is the total amount of light collected by the camera's sensor during a single shutter cycle. A *shutter cycle* occurs when the Shutter Release button is pressed, the shutter opens, closes, and resets. One shutter cycle occurs for each image (with the exception of multiple exposures, of course). An exposure is made of three elements that are all interrelated. Each depends on the others to create a proper exposure. If one of the elements changes, the others must increase or decrease proportionally or you will no longer have an equivalent exposure. The following are the elements you need to consider.

▶ **Shutter speed.** The shutter speed determines the length of time the sensor is exposed to light.

▶ **ISO sensitivity.** The ISO setting you choose influences your camera's sensitivity to light.

▶ **Aperture/f-stop.** How much light reaches the sensor of your camera is controlled by the aperture, or f-stop. Each camera has an adjustable opening on the lens. As you change the aperture (the opening), you allow more or less light to reach the sensor.

Shutter speed

Shutter speed is the amount of time that light entering from the lens is allowed to expose the image sensor. Obviously, if the shutter is open longer, more light can reach the sensor. The shutter speed can also affect the sharpness of your images. When handholding the camera and using a longer focal-length lens, a faster shutter speed is often required to counteract against camera shake from hand movement, which can cause blur (this is the effect that VR lenses were made to combat). When taking photographs in low light, a slow shutter speed is often required, which also causes blur from camera shake and/or fast-moving subjects.

The shutter speed can also be used to effectively show motion in photography. Panning, or moving the camera horizontally with a moving subject, while using a slower shutter speed can cause the background to blur while keeping the subject in focus. This is an effective way to portray motion in a still image. On the opposite end, using a fast shutter speed can freeze action such as the splash of the wave of a surfer, which can also give the illusion of motion in a still photograph.

Shutter speeds are indicated in fractions of a second. Common shutter speeds (from slow to fast) are: 1 second, 1/2, 1/4, 1/8, 1/15, 1/30, 1/60, 1/125, 1/250, 1/500, 1/1000, and so on. Increasing or decreasing shutter speed by one setting doubles or halves the exposure, respectively. The D3000 also allows you to adjust the shutter speed in 1/3-stops. It may seem like math (okay, technically it does involve math), but it is relatively easy to figure out. For example, if you take a picture with a 1/2-second shutter speed and it turns out too dark, logically you'll want to keep the shutter open longer to let in more light. To do this, you need to adjust the shutter speed to 1 second, which is the next full stop, letting in twice as much light.

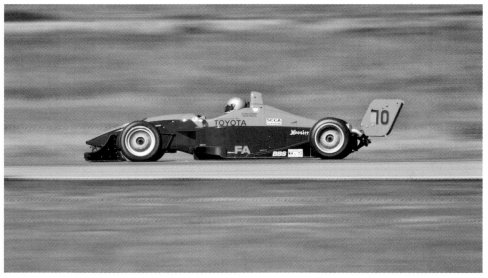

4.1 For this image I used a relatively slow shutter speed of 1/100 second and panning to blur the background providing an element of speed and movement to the photo.

ISO

The ISO is what used to commonly be referred to as "film speed" in photography. Generally these days it is referred to as "sensitivity" or even just simply called ISO. The term *ISO* is derived from the International Organization for Standardization, which is a sort of a governing body in the international manufacturing markets. The International Organization for Standardization allows for the consumers to be able to buy similar products from different manufacturers while knowing that the product will perform in the same manner. As it relates to photography, this allowed photographers to purchase different brands of film knowing that the settings used on 100-speed Kodak film would be the same settings used in equivalent light with 100-speed Fuji film.

In addition, the ISO sensitivity number also tells how sensitive to light the medium is; in this case, the medium being the CCD sensor. The higher the ISO number is, the more sensitive it is and the less light you need to take a photograph. For example, you might choose an ISO setting of 100 on a bright, sunny day when you are photographing outside because you have plenty of light. However, on a cloudy day you may want to consider an ISO of 400 to make sure your camera captures all the available light. This allows you to use a faster shutter speed should it be appropriate to the subject you are photographing.

It is helpful to know that each ISO setting is twice as sensitive to light as the previous setting. For example, at ISO 400 your camera is twice as sensitive to light as it is at ISO 200. This means it needs only half the light at ISO 400 that it needs at ISO 200 to achieve the same exposure.

Aperture

Aperture is the size of the opening in the lens that determines the amount of light that reaches the image sensor. The aperture is controlled by a metal diaphragm that operates in a similar fashion to the iris of your eye. Aperture is expressed as f-stop numbers, such as f/2.8, f/4, f/5.6, and f/8. Here are a couple of important things to know about aperture:

▶ **Smaller f-numbers equal wider apertures.** A small f-stop such as f/2.8, for example, opens the lens so more light reaches the sensor. If you have a wide aperture (opening), the amount of time the shutter needs to stay open to let light into the camera decreases.

▶ **Larger f-numbers equal narrower apertures.** A large f-stop such as f/11, for example, closes the lens so less light reaches the sensor. If you have a narrow aperture (opening), the amount of time the shutter needs to stay open to let light into the camera increases.

I often get asked why the numbers of the aperture seem to be counterintuitive. The answer is relatively simple; the numbers are actually derived from ratios, which translate into fractions. The f-number is defined by the focal length of the lens divided by the actual diameter of the aperture opening. The simplest way to look at it is to put a 1 on top of the f-number as the numerator. For the simplest example, take a 50mm f/2 lens (okay, Nikon doesn't actually make a 50mm f/2, but let's pretend for a minute).

Take the aperture number, f/2, and add 1 as the numerator. You get 1/2. This indicates that the aperture opening is half the diameter of the focal length, 25mm. So at f/4 the effective diameter of the aperture is 12.5mm. It's a pretty simple concept once you break it down.

The terms *aperture* and *f-stop* are interchangeable.

As with ISO and shutter speed there are standard settings for aperture, each of which is 1 stop difference from the other. The standard f-numbers are f/1.4, f/2, f/2.8, f/4, f/5.6, f/8, f/11, f/16, and f/22. At first glance these may appear to be a random assortment of numbers, but they aren't. Upon closer inspection you notice that every other number is a multiple of 2. When you break it down even further you find that each stop is a multiple of 1.4. This is where the standard f-stop numbers are derived from. Starting out with f/1; multiply by 1.4. You get f/1.4. Again multiply by 1.4; you get 2. Multiply by 1.4; you get 2.8, and so on.

| f/1.4 | f/2 | f/2.8 | f/4 | f/5.6 | f/8 | f/11 | f/16 |

4.2 This shows the relative difference in aperture sizes.

Similar to the shutter speed settings, the Nikon D3000 also allows you to set the aperture in 1/3-stop increments.

In photographic vernacular, *opening up* refers to going from a smaller to a larger aperture and *stopping down* refers to going from a larger to smaller aperture.

Now that you know a little more about apertures, you can begin to look at why different aperture settings are used and the effect that they have on your images. The most common reason why a certain aperture is selected is to control the depth of field or how much of the image is in focus. Quite simply, using a wider aperture (f/1.4 – 4) gives you a shallow depth of field allowing you to exercise *selective focus;* this allows you to focus on a certain subject in the image while allowing the rest to fall out of focus. Conversely, using a small aperture (f/11-32) maximizes your depth of field, allowing you to get everything in focus. Using a wider aperture is generally preferable when shooting portraits to blur the background and draw attention to the subject, and a smaller aperture is generally used when photographing landscapes to ensure that the whole scene is in focus. Depth of field is discussed in more detail later in this chapter.

Another way that the aperture setting is used is, oddly enough, to control the shutter speed. When selecting an aperture, you can use a wide aperture to allow a lot of light in so that you can user a faster shutter speed to freeze action. On the opposite end of the spectrum, you can use a smaller aperture if you want to be sure that your shutter speed is slower.

Fine-Tuning Your Exposure

Your camera's meter may not always be completely accurate. There are a lot of variables in most scenes, and large bright or dark areas can trick the meter into thinking a scene is brighter or

4.3 This shot of my Boston terrier Henrietta was shot with a wide aperture of f/1.4 to achieve a shallow depth of field.

darker than it really is, causing the image to be over- or underexposed. One example of this is in a really bright situation such as the beach on a sunny day or a similar, albeit opposite weather-wise, snowy scene. The camera's meter generally sees all of the brightness in the scene and will underexpose to try to preserve detail in the highlights causing the main subject and most of the image to be dark and lacking in contrast. In snowy scenes, this is a special problem because it causes the snow to appear gray and dingy. The general rule of thumb in this situation is to add 1 to 2 stops of exposure compensation.

Exposure compensation is not available when using scene modes.

Exposure compensation

Exposure compensation is a feature of the D3000 that allows you to fine-tune the amount of exposure to vary from what is set by the camera's exposure meter. Although you can usually adjust the exposure of the image in your image-editing software (especially if you shoot RAW), it's best to get the exposure right in the camera to be sure that you have the highest image quality. If after taking the photograph, you review it and it's too dark or too light, you can adjust the exposure compensation and retake the picture to get a better exposure. Exposure compensation is adjusted in EV (Exposure Value); 1 EV is equal to 1 stop of light. You adjust exposure compensation by pressing the Exposure Compensation button, next to the Shutter Release button (the button with the +/-), and rotating the Command dial to the left for more exposure (+EV) or to the right for less exposure (–EV). The exposure compensation is adjusted in 1/3 stops of light.

You can adjust the exposure compensation up to +5 EV and down to –5 EV, which is a large range of 10 stops. To remind you that exposure compensation has been set, the exposure compensation indicator is displayed in the viewfinder and on the rear LCD screen when the shooting info is being displayed.

 CAUTION Be sure to reset the exposure compensation to 0 after you finish to avoid unwanted over- or underexposure.

There are a few ways to get the exact exposure that you want. You can use the histogram to determine whether you need to add or subtract from your exposure. You can also use bracketing to take a number of exposures and choose from the one that you think is best, or you can combine the bracketed images with different exposures to create one image using post-processing software.

Histograms

The easiest way to determine if you need to adjust the exposure compensation is to simply preview your image. If it looks too dark, add some exposure compensation; if it's too bright, adjust the exposure compensation down. This, however, is not the most accurate method of determining how much exposure compensation to use. To accurately determine how much exposure compensation to add or subtract, look at the *histogram*. A histogram is a visual representation of the tonal values in your image. Think of it as a bar graph that charts the lights, darks, and midtones in your picture.

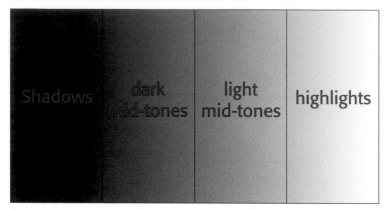

4.4 A representation of the tonal range of a histogram

The histogram charts a tonal range of about 5 stops, which is about the limit of what the D3000's sensor can record. This range is broken down into 256 brightness levels from 0 (absolute black) to 255 (absolute white), with 128 coming in at middle or 18 percent gray. The more pixels there are at any given brightness value, the higher the bar. If there are no bars, then the image has no pixels in that brightness range.

The D3000 offers four histogram views: the luminance histogram, which shows the brightness levels of the entire image, and histograms for each color channel — red, green, and blue.

The most useful histogram for determining if your exposure needs adjusting is the luminance histogram. To display the luminance histogram, simply press the Multi-selector up while viewing the image on the LCD. This displays a thumbnail of the current image, the shooting info, and a small luminance histogram.

Ideally, you want to expose your subject so that it falls right about in the middle of the tonal range, which is why your camera's meter exposes for 18 percent gray. If your histogram graph has most of the information bunched up on the left side, then your image is probably underexposed; if it's bunched up on the right side, then your image is probably overexposed. Ideally, with most average subjects that aren't bright white or extremely dark, you want to try to get your histogram to look sort of like a bell curve, with most of the tones in the middle range, tapering off as they get to the dark and light ends of the graph. But this is only for most average types of images. As with almost everything in photography, there are exceptions to the rule. If you take a photo of a dark subject on a dark background (a low-key image), then naturally your histogram will have most of the tones bunched up on the left side of the graph. Conversely, when you take a photograph of a light subject on a light background (a high-key image), the histogram will have most of the tones bunched up to the right.

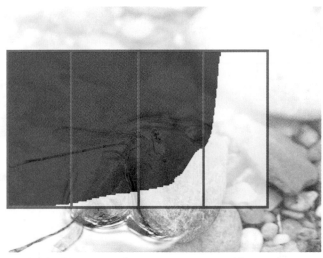

4.5 An example of a histogram from an overexposed image (no highlight detail). Notice the graph is completely touching far right of the graph.

The most important thing to remember is that there is no such thing as a perfect histogram. A histogram is just a factual representation of the tones in the image. The other important thing to remember is that although it's okay for the graph to be near one side or the other, you usually don't want your histogram to have spikes bumping up against the edge of the graph; this indicates your image has blown-out highlights (completely white, with no detail) or blocked-up shadow areas (completely black, with no detail).

4.6 An example of a histogram from an underexposed image (no shadow detail). Notice the spikes at the far left of the graph.

**4.7 An example of a histogram from a properly exposed image.
Notice that the graph does not spike against the edge on the left or
the right, but tapers off.**

4.8 An example of a histogram from a low-key image

4.9 An example of a histogram from a high-key image

Now that you know a little bit about histograms, you can use them to adjust exposure compensation. Here is a good set of steps to follow when using the histogram as a tool to evaluate your photos:

1. **After taking your picture, review its histogram on the LCD.** To view the histogram in the image preview, press the Playback button to view the image. Press the Multi-selector up, and the histogram appears directly to the right of the image preview.

2. **Look at the histogram.** An example of an ideal histogram can be seen in figure 4.7.

3. **Adjust the exposure compensation.** To move the tones to the right and make the image brighter, add a little exposure compensation by pressing the Exposure Compensation button and rotating the Command dial to the left. To move the tones to the left and darken the image, press the Exposure Compensation button and rotate the Command dial to the right.

4. **Retake the photograph if necessary.** After taking another picture, review the histogram again. If needed, adjust the exposure compensation more until you achieve the desired exposure.

Bracketing

Another way to ensure that you get the proper exposure is to *bracket* your exposures. Bracketing is a photographic technique in which you vary the exposure of your subject over three or more frames. By doing this, you are able to get the proper exposure in difficult lighting situations where your camera's meter can be fooled. Bracketing is usually done with at least one exposure under and one exposure over the metered exposure.

Although some Nikon dSLRs offer an auto-bracketing feature, the D3000 doesn't. It's not a big deal, however; it's almost as easy to bracket images manually. It's a very simple procedure to do.

1. **Set the exposure mode to Manual.**

2. **Using the exposure meter set the aperture and shutter speed so that you getting the proper exposure.** A typical exposure on a sunny day will be f/16 at 1/125 second at ISO 100.

3. **Take a shot at the proper exposure.**

4. **Adjust your settings.** You can now change the exposure setting. A good start is to adjust your exposure settings by at least one stop.

5. **Take multiple shots.** You'll want to take both overexposed and underexposed images.

When bracketing, whether you adjust the shutter speed or aperture depends on what kind of picture you are taking. If there's a lot of movement in the scene, you probably want to change the aperture. If depth of field is a concern, you want to change the shutter speed.

In addition to helping ensure that you get the correct exposure, you can also use different elements from the bracketed exposures and combine them using image-editing software to get a final image that has a wider tonal range than is possible for your image sensor to capture. This technique is known as High Dynamic Range (HDR). You can use a few different programs to create an HDR image. Photoshop CS2, CS3, and CS4, have a tool called Merge to HDR that enables you to select two or more images (using three to five images is recommended) and automatically merges the separate images for you. Using Photoshop you can also layer the bracketed images and use layer masks to reveal or hide different areas of the images. Although HDR is a very good tool for getting more tonal range in your images, be careful not to overuse it. In recent years, quite a few photographers have had the tendency to take this technology too far, creating unrealistic, overly processed-looking images.

Figures 4.10, 4.11, and 4.12 are a sequence of bracketed images. I bracketed 3 frames by one stop to show the broad range of exposures you can get with bracketing. Figure 4.13 is a composite of all three images used to create an HDR image.

4.10 Bracketed image underexposed by 1 stop

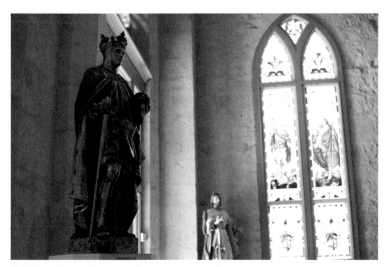

4.11 Bracketed image shot as metered

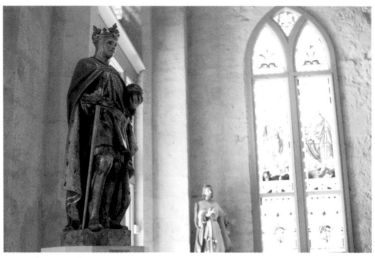

4.12 Bracketed image overexposed by 1 stop

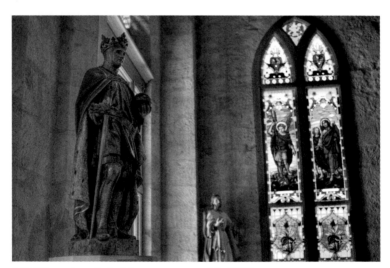

4.13 Three bracketed images merged to HDR

Understanding Depth of Field

Depth of field is the distance range in a photograph in which all included portions of an image are at least acceptably sharp. It is heavily affected by aperture, but how far your camera is from the subject also has an effect as does the focal length of the lens.

Remember that wide-angle lenses give a deeper depth of field at a given aperture and distance than lenses with longer focal lengths at the same settings.

If you focus your lens on a certain point, everything that lies on the horizontal plane of that same distance is also in focus. This means everything in front of the point and everything behind it is technically not in focus. Because our eyes aren't acute enough to discern the minor blur that occurs directly in front of and directly behind the point of focus, it still appears sharp to us. This is known as the zone of acceptable sharpness, which we call depth of field.

▶ **Shallow depth of field.** This results in an image where the subject is in sharp focus, but the background and/or the foreground has a soft blur. You likely have seen it used frequently in portraits. Using a wide aperture, such as f/2.8, results in a subject that is sharp with a softer background. Using a shallow depth of field is a great way to get rid of distracting elements in the background of an image.

▶ **Deep depth of field.** This results in an image that is reasonably sharp from the foreground to the background. Using a narrow aperture such as f/11 is ideal to keep photographs of landscapes or groups in focus throughout.

4.14 An image with a shallow depth of field has only the main subject in focus.

4.15 An image with a deep depth of field has most of the image in focus.

A factor to consider when working with depth of field is your distance from the subject. The farther you are from the subject you are focusing on the greater the depth of field in your photograph. For example, if you stand in your front yard to take a photo of a tree a block away, it has a deep depth of field with the tree, background, and foreground all in relatively sharp focus. If you stand in the same spot and take a picture of your dog that is standing just several feet away, your dog is in focus, but that tree a block away is just a blur of color.

 To get deep depth of field, use a higher aperture number; to get a shallow depth of field, use a smaller aperture number.

Rules of Composition

Although some of you are likely well versed in the concepts of composition, some of you may be coming in cold, so to speak. So this section is intended as a refresher course and a general outline of some of the most commonly used rules of composition.

Photography, like any artistic discipline, has general rules. Although they are called rules, they are really nothing more than guidelines. Some photographers — notably Ansel Adams, who was quoted as saying, "The so-called rules of photographic composition are, in my opinion, invalid, irrelevant, and immaterial" — claim to have eschewed the rules of composition. However, when you look at Adams's photographs, they follow the rules perfectly in most cases.

Another famous photographer, Edward Weston, said, "Consulting the rules of composition before taking a photograph is like consulting the laws of gravity before going for a walk." Again, as with Adams, when you look at his photographs, they tend to follow these very rules.

This isn't to say you need to follow all the rules every time you take a photograph. As I said, these are really just general guidelines that when followed can make your images more powerful and interesting.

However, when you're starting out in photography, you should pay attention to the rules of composition. Eventually, you become accustomed to following the guidelines and it becomes second nature. At that point you no longer need to consult the rules of composition; you just inherently follow them.

Keep it simple

Simplicity is arguably the most important rule in creating a good image. In most cases, you want to be sure the viewer can identify what the intended subject of your photograph is. When you have too many competing elements in your image, it can be hard for the viewer to decide what to focus on.

One of the most commonly used techniques for achieving simplicity in images is to frame a single subject against a plain backdrop. Another much-used technique is using a shallow depth of field to isolate the subject from a background that may be busy. By causing the background to go out of focus the subject stands out better.

4.16 There's no question as to what the subject is in this photograph.

Sometimes changing your perspective to the subject is all you need to do to remove a distracting element from your image. A good tip is to try walking around and shooting the same subject from different angles.

Simplicity in an image can speak volumes. Try to concentrate on removing any unnecessary elements to achieve simplicity.

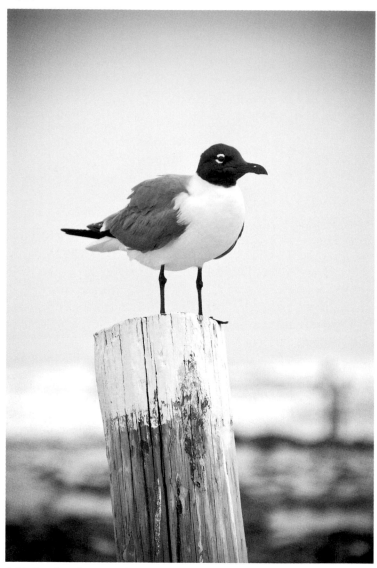

4.17 Getting down and shooting this seagull from a lower angle allowed me to place the sky behind him. Shooting the bird from up high would have placed the distracting elements of the beach behind the main subject of the photo.

Rule of Thirds

Beginning photographers are often likely to take the main subject of the photograph and stick it right in the middle of the frame. This seems to makes sense, and it often works pretty well for snapshots. However, your goal is to create more interesting and dynamic images, so it often works better to put the main subject of the image a little off-center. Placing the subject off-center in a random position also rarely works to make a good composition. Fortunately there is what is known as *"the Rule of Thirds."*

The Rule of Thirds is a compositional guideline that has been in use for hundreds of years, and famous artists throughout the centuries have followed it. With the Rule of Thirds, you divide the image into nine equal parts using two equally spaced horizontal and vertical lines, kind of like a tic-tac-toe pattern. You want to center the main subject of the image at an intersection, as illustrated in figure 4.18. The subject doesn't neces-sarily have to be right on the intersection of the line, but merely close enough to it to take advantage of the Rule of Thirds.

Another way to use the Rule of Thirds is to place the subject in the center of the frame, but at the bottom or top third of the frame. This part of the rule is especially useful when photographing landscapes. You can place the horizon on or near the top or bottom line, but you almost never want to place it in the middle. Of course, there are always exceptions so if you think that the subject might look better in the middle by all means give it a shot. It never hurts to experiment, and it's better to have tried a shot and failed than not tried it at all.

4.18 The guitarist Jimmie Vaughan, who is the main subject of this photograph, is placed to the left of the frame according to the Rule of Thirds.

When using the Rule of Thirds with a moving subject, you want to be sure to keep most of the frame in front of the subject to present the illusion that the subject has someplace to go within the frame.

Leading lines and S-curves

Another good way to add drama to an image is to use a *leading line* to draw the viewer's eye through the picture. A leading line is an element in a composition that leads the eye toward the subject. A leading line can be a lot of different things: a road, sidewalk, railroad tracks, buildings, or columns, to name a few.

In general, you want your leading line to go in a specific direction. Most commonly, a leading line leads the eye from one corner of the picture to another. A good rule of thumb to follow is to have your line go from the bottom-left corner leading toward the top right.

You can also use leading lines that go from the bottom of the image to the top, and vice versa. Often, leading lines heading in this direction lead to a *vanishing point*. A vanishing point is the point at which parallel lines appear to converge and disappear. Figure 4.19 shows a leading line ending in a vanishing point. Depending on the subject matter, a variety of directions for leading lines can work equally well.

4.19 A leading line draws the viewer's eye through the image.

Another nice way to use a leading line is with an *S-curve.* An S-curve is exactly what it sounds like: It resembles the letter S. The S-curve draws the viewer's eye up from the bottom of the image, through the middle, over to the corner, and back to the other side again.

Helpful hints

Along with the major rules of composition, there are all sorts of other helpful guidelines. Here are just a few that I've found most helpful:

- ▶ **Frame the subject.** Use elements of the foreground to make a frame around the subject to keep the viewer's eye from wandering.

- ▶ **Avoid having the subject looking directly out of the side of the frame he is closest to.** Having the subject looking out of the photograph can be distracting to the viewer. For example, if your subject is on the left side of the composition having him face the right is better, and vice versa.

- ▶ **Avoid *mergers*.** A merger is when an element from the background appears to be a part of the subject, like the snapshot of granny at the park that looks like she has a tree growing out of the top of her head.

- ▶ **Try not to cut through the joint of a limb.** When composing or cropping your picture, it's best not to end the frame on a joint, such as an elbow or a knee. This can be unsettling to the viewer.

- ▶ **Avoid having bright spots or unnecessary details near the edge.** Having anything bright or detailed near the edge of the frame will draw the viewer's eye away from the subject and out of the image.

- ▶ **Avoid placing the horizon or strong horizontal or vertical lines in the center of the composition.** This cuts the image in half and makes it hard for the viewer to decide which half of the image is important.

- ▶ **Separate the subject from the background.** Make sure the background doesn't have colors or textures similar to the subject. If necessary, try shooting from different angles, or use a shallow depth of field to achieve separation.

- ▶ **Fill the frame.** Try to make the subject the most dominant part of the image. Avoid having lots of empty space around the subject unless it's essential to making the photograph work.

- ▶ **Use odd numbers.** When photographing multiple subjects, odd numbers seem to work best.

These are just a few of the hundreds of guidelines out there. Remember, these are not hard-and-fast rules, just simple pointers that can help you create interesting and amazing images.

CHAPTER 5

Selecting and Using Lenses

The lens that you put on your camera is almost as important as the camera body. Some may argue that the lens is more important than the actual camera. There are many different types of lenses, from ultrawide-angle lenses to super-telephoto lenses. The lens that you use depends on the subject you're photographing, as well as how you want the subject to appear in your images. The different types of lenses all have an impact on the way the subject looks to the viewer. You have a lot to consider when purchasing a lens, whether it's a zoom or prime lens, a wide-angle or telephoto lens, or any of the numerous other options. The goal of this chapter is to give you a head start on knowing what kind of lens you want before you actually start looking.

The ability to use a variety of lenses is one of the main advantages of using a dSLR camera.

Nikon Lens Compatibility

One thing you need to remember before purchasing a lens for your D3000 is that only Nikon AF-S (or the third-party equivalent) lenses autofocus with the D3000. Until recently, all Nikon AF lenses were focused by a screw-type motor in the camera body. Most high-level cameras have this focus motor, but some models leave it out to make the cameras more compact; the D3000 is one such model.

 Sigma's AF-S equivalent is termed HSM for Hyper-Sonic Motor.

AF-S lenses are focused by an internal mechanism in the lens that uses ultrasonic vibrations to drive the focus motor. This eliminates the need for an external motor to move the lens elements and also makes for very quiet and fast autofocus. Previous to the AF-S lens, Nikon offered AF-I lenses that worked on the same principle. These lenses also autofocus with the D3000.

Although AF-S lenses such as the kit lens are the only lenses that offer full AF functionality, almost any Nikon lens made since 1977 can mount to the camera and offers some, but not all, available features.

Any AF-D or AF-G lens allows all functions (except AF, of course). Any lens that doesn't have a CPU (non-CPU) does not autofocus, nor does the exposure meter work. Metering has to be done by using an external light meter or estimation and you have to shoot in Manual exposure mode. All non-CPU lenses are manual focus lenses, but some manual focus lenses have a CPU; these lenses are known as AI-P. With AI-P lenses, all features are available, except AF and 3D Color Matrix metering.

Deciphering Nikon's Lens Codes

When shopping for lenses, you may notice all sorts of letter designations in the lens name. For example, the kit lens is the AF-S DX Nikkor 18-55mm f/3.5-5.6G ED VR. So, what do all those letters mean? Here's a simple list to help you decipher them:

▶ **AI/AIS.** These are auto-indexing lenses that automatically adjust the aperture diaphragm down when the Shutter Release button is pressed. All lenses made after 1977 are auto-indexing, but when referring to AI lenses, most people generally mean the older Manual Focus (MF) lenses.

▶ **E.** These lenses were Nikon's budget series lenses, made to go with the lower-end film cameras, such as the EM, FG, and FG-20. Although these lenses are compact and are often constructed with plastic parts, some of them, especially the 50mm f/1.8, are of quite good quality. These lenses are also manual focus only.

▶ **D.** Lenses with this designation convey distance information to the camera to aid in metering for exposure and flash.

▶ **G.** These are newer lenses that lack a manually adjustable aperture ring. You must set the aperture on the camera body.

▶ **AF, AF-D, AF-I, and AF-S.** All these lens codes denote that the lens is an auto-focus (AF) lens. The AF-D represents a distance encoder for distance information, the AF-I indicates an internal focusing motor type, and the AF-S indicates an internal Silent Wave Motor.

▶ **AI-P.** This designates a manual focus lens that has a CPU chip.

▶ **DX.** This lets you know the lens was optimized for use with Nikon's DX-format sensor. The DX designation is explained in depth in the next section.

▶ **VR.** This code denotes that the lens is equipped with Nikon's Vibration Reduction image stabilization system.

▶ **ED.** This indicates that some of the glass in the lens is Nikon's Extra-Low Dispersion glass, which means the lens is less prone to lens flare and chromatic aberrations. Chromatic aberrations can be seen as color fringing around the edges of a high contrast subject. These are usually more pronounced at the edges of the images.

▶ **Micro-Nikkor.** Even though they're labeled as micro, these are Nikon's macro lenses.

▶ **IF.** IF stands for internal focus. The focusing mechanism is inside the lens, so the front of the lens doesn't rotate or move in and out when focusing. This feature is useful when you don't want the front of the lens element to move — for example, when you use a polarizing filter. The internal focus mechanism also allows for faster focusing.

▶ **DC.** DC stands for Defocus Control. Nikon only offers a couple of lenses with this designation. These lenses make the out-of-focus areas in the image appear softer by using special lens elements to add spherical aberration. The parts of the image that are in focus aren't affected. Currently, the only Nikon lenses with this feature are the 135mm f/2 and the 105mm f/2. Both of these are considered portrait lenses.

▶ **N.** On some of Nikon's newest professional lenses, you may see a large, golden N. This means that the lens has Nikon's Nano Crystal Coating, which is designed to reduce flare and ghosting.

DX Crop Factor

Crop factor is a ratio that describes the size of a camera's imaging area as compared to another format; in the case of SLR cameras, the reference format is 35mm film.

SLR camera lenses were designed around the 35mm film format. Photographers use lenses of a certain focal length to provide a specific field of view. The field of view, also called the angle of view, is the amount of the scene that's captured in an image. This is usually described in degrees. For example, when you use a 16mm lens on a 35mm camera, it captures almost 180 degrees of the scene horizontally, which is quite a bit. Conversely, when you use a 300mm focal length, the field of view is reduced to a mere 6.5 degrees horizontally, which is a very small part of the scene. The field of view is consistent from camera to camera because all SLRs use 35mm film, which has an image area of 24mm × 36mm.

With the advent of digital SLRs, the sensor was made smaller than a frame of 35mm film to keep costs down because the sensors are more expensive to manufacture. This sensor size was called APS-C or, in Nikon terms, the DX-format. The lenses that are used with DX-format dSLRs have the same focal length they've always had, but because the sensor doesn't have the same amount of area as the film, the field of view is effectively decreased. This causes the lens to provide the field of view of a longer focal lens when compared to 35mm film images.

5.1 This image was shot with a 28mm lens on a D700 FX camera. Inside the red square is the amount of the scene that would be captured with the same lens on a DX camera like the D3000.

Fortunately, the DX sensors are a uniform size, thereby supplying consumers with a standard to determine how much the field of view is reduced on a DX-format dSLR with any lens. The digital sensors in Nikon DX cameras have a 1.5X crop factor, which means that to determine the equivalent focal length of a 35mm or FX camera, you simply have to multiply the focal length of the lens by 1.5. Therefore, a 28mm lens provides an angle of coverage similar to a 42mm lens, a 50mm is equivalent to a 75mm, and so on.

Early on, when dSLRs were first introduced, all lenses were based on 35mm film. The crop factor effectively reduced the coverage of these lenses, causing ultrawide-angle lenses to act like wide-angle lenses, wide-angle lenses to perform like normal lenses, normal lenses to provide the same coverage as short telephotos, and so on. Nikon created specific lenses for dSLRs with digital sensors. These lenses are known as DX-format lenses. The focal length of these lenses was shortened to fill the gap to allow true super-wide-angle lenses. These DX-format lenses were also redesigned to cast a smaller image inside the camera so that the lenses could actually be made smaller and use less glass than conventional lenses. The byproduct of designing a lens to project an image circle to a smaller sensor is that these same lenses can't effectively be used with FX-format and can't be used at all with 35mm film cameras (without severe vignetting) because the image won't completely fill an area the size of the film or FX sensor.

There is an upside to this crop factor. Lenses with longer focal lengths now provide a bit of extra reach. A lens set at 200mm now provides the same amount of coverage as a 300mm lens, which can offer a great advantage for sports and wildlife photography or when you simply can't get close enough to your subject.

Detachable Lenses

Although your D3000 comes with a kit lens — the 18-55mm f/3.5-5.6G VR — one advantage to owning a digital SLR camera is the ability to use detachable lenses. This allows you to change your lens to fit the specific photographic style or scene that you want to capture. After a while, you may find that the kit lens doesn't meet your needs and you want to upgrade. Nikon dSLR owners have quite a few lenses from which to choose, all of which benefit from Nikon's expertise in the field of lens manufacturing.

One of the great things about photography is that through your lens choice, you can show things in a way that the human eye can't perceive. The human eye is basically a fixed-focal-length lens. We can only see a certain set angular distance. This is called our *field of view* (or angle of view). Our eyes have about the same field of view as a 35mm lens on your D3000. Changing the focal length of your lens, whether by switching lenses or zooming, changes the field of view, allowing the camera to "see" more or less of the scene that you're photographing. Changing the focal length of the lens allows you to change the perspective of your images. In the following sections, I discuss the different types of lenses and how they can influence the subjects that you're photographing.

Kit Lenses

The Nikon D3000 comes paired with Nikon's 18-55mm f/3.5-5.6G VR AF-S DX lens that was first offered coupled with the D60. This lens covers the most commonly used focal lengths for everyday photography. The 18mm setting covers the wide-angle range, and zooming all the way out to 55mm gives you a moderate telephoto setting, allowing you to get close-up photos of subjects that may not be very close. Nikon also offers a D3000 kit with two lenses, the 18-55mm and a 55-200mm f/4-5.6 AF-S DX VR. The 55-200mm lens allows you a good medium-to-long telephoto range to really pull those far-off subjects closer, and it offers Nikon's Vibration Reduction (VR) feature. This feature allows you to handhold the camera at slower shutter speeds without worrying about image blur that can be caused by camera shake.

This lens has received many good reviews. The optics give you sharp images with good contrast when stopped down a bit. However, when shooting wide open, the images can appear a little soft around the corners. It should be said here that all lenses have a "sweet spot" or a range of apertures at which they appear sharpest. With most lenses this sweet spot is usually one or two stops from the maximum aperture. For the kit lens, the sweet spot is around f/5.6 to f/8. Another thing to be aware of is that as the aperture gets smaller than f/16, you also may lose some sharpness due to the diffraction of the light by the aperture blades.

 Stopping down refs to making the aperture smaller, and *opening up* refers to making the aperture larger.

Although Nikon offers many very high-quality professional lenses, the D3000 kit lenses are very good performers for their price range, and they offer some advantages when paired with the D3000 that even some of Nikon's more expensive lenses don't. These advantages include the following:

▶ **Low cost.** The 18-55mm VR lens costs less than $200, while the 55-200mm VR lens comes in at around $250. The 18-200mm VR lens retails for around $750. Buying both the 18-55mm and 55-200mm VR lenses can save you around $300.

▶ **Superior image quality.** These lenses offer very high quality for the price. They offer aspherical lens elements, which help to eliminate distortion, and Nikon's Super Integrated Coating on the lens helps to ensure accurate color and reduce lens flare. These lenses have been praised by professional and amateur reviewers alike. They are uncommonly sharp for a lens in this price range.

▶ **Compact size.** Being designed specifically for dSLR cameras, these lenses are small in size and super-light. They are great lenses for everyday use or long trips where you don't want a lot of gear weighing you down.

▶ **VR.** Vibration Reduction is a very handy feature, especially when working in low-light situations or when using a long focal length. It can allow you to handhold your camera at slower shutter speeds than you can with standard lenses.

Image courtesy of Nikon, Inc.
5.2 The D3000 with the 18-55mm kit lens

Zoom Lenses versus Prime Lenses

This debate has been a hot topic for many years. In the past eight years or so, lens technology has grown by leaps and bounds, and zoom lenses are just about as sharp as primes or, in the case of the Nikkor 14-24mm f/2.8, even sharper than most primes. Some photographers prefer primes, and some prefer zooms. It's largely a personal choice, and there are some things to consider.

Understanding zoom lenses

A zoom lens, such as the AF-S Nikkor 14-24mm, is a lens that has multiple optical elements that move within the lens body; this allows the lens to change focal length, and therefore field of view, which is how much of the scene you can see at any given focal length.

One of the main advantages of the zoom lens is its versatility. You can attach one lens to your camera and use it in a wide variety of situations.

There are a few things to consider when buying zoom lenses (or upgrading from one you already have), including variable aperture, depth of field, and quality.

Variable aperture

One of the major issues when buying a consumer-level lens such as the 18-55mm VR lens is that it has a variable aperture, which means that as you zoom in on something when shooting wide open or closed down to the minimum aperture, the aperture opening gets smaller, allowing less light to reach the sensor and causing the need for a slower shutter speed or higher ISO setting. More high-end lenses have a constant aperture all the way through the zoom range. In daylight or brightly lit situations, this may not be a factor, but when shooting in low light, this can be a drawback. Although the VR feature helps when shooting relatively still subjects, moving subjects in low light are blurred.

If you do a lot of low-light shooting of moving subjects, such as concert photography, you may want to look into getting a zoom lens with a wider aperture such as f/2.8. These are fast aperture pro lenses and usually cost quite a bit more than your standard consumer zoom lens. The lens I use most when photographing action in low light is the Nikkor 17-55mm f/2.8; this lens allows me to use an ISO of about 800 (keeping the noise levels low) and relatively fast shutter speeds to freeze the motion of the subject.

☐ : Nano Crystal Coat   ▨ : Aspherical lens elements

☐ : ED glass elements

5.3 Lenses are made up of many different glass elements. This is a diagram of the inside of a Nikon 14 24mm f/2.8 lens.

Depth of field

Another consideration when buying a zoom lens is depth of field. For example, the 18-55mm lens gives you more depth of field at all focal lengths than a lens with a wider aperture. If you are shooting landscapes, this may not be a problem, but if you are getting into portrait photography, you may want a shallower depth of field; therefore, a lens with a wider aperture is probably what you want.

Quality

In order to make consumer lenses like the 18-55mm VR and the 55-200mm VR afford-able, Nikon makes them mostly out of a composite plastic. Although the build quality is pretty good, the higher-end lenses have metal lens mounts and some have metal alloy lens bodies. This makes them a lot more durable in the long run, especially if you are rough on your gear like I sometimes am. Conversely, the plastic bodies of the consumer lenses are much smaller and lighter than their pro-level counterparts. This is a great feature when traveling or if you want to pack light. If I'm going on a trip, more often than not, I'll just grab my D3000 kit and go. It's more compact and much lighter than my other cameras and lenses and I appreciate the small size.

Understanding prime lenses

Before zoom lenses were available, the only option a photographer had was using a prime lens, which is also called a fixed-focal-length lens. Because each lens is fixed at a certain focal length, when the photographer wants to change how much of the scene is in the image, he has to either physically move farther away from or closer to the subject, or swap out the lens with one that has a focal length more suited to the range.

The most important features of the prime lens are that they offer a faster maximum aperture, they are generally far lighter, and they cost much less. The normal focal length prime lenses aren't very long, so the maximum aperture can be faster than with zoom lenses. Prime lenses in normal focal lengths also require fewer lens elements and moving parts, so the weight can be kept down considerably; and because there are fewer elements, the overall cost of production is less; therefore, you pay less.

One might say, "Well, if I can buy one zoom lens that encompasses the same range as four or five prime lenses, then why bother with prime lenses?" While this may sound logical, there are a lot of reasons why you might choose a prime lens over a zoom lens.

Prime lenses don't require as many lens elements (pieces of glass) as zoom lenses do, and this means that prime lenses are almost always sharper than zoom lenses. The differences in optical quality are not as noticeable as they were in the past, but with digital camera resolutions getting higher, the differences are definitely becoming more noticeable.

Image courtesy of Nikon, Inc.

5.4 The Nikkor 35mm f/1.8G AF-S fixed-focal-length prime lens

As discussed earlier in the chapter, the Nikon D3000 can only autofocus when an AF-S lens is attached to the camera. At this time, Nikon only offers a limited number of AF-S prime lenses and most of them tend to be somewhat expensive and have longer focal lengths. Currently, the AF-S prime lens lineup consists of the 35mm f/1.8, 50mm f/1.4, 60mm f/2.8 macro, and 105mm f/2.8 VR macro. For telephoto primes, you have the 200mm, 300mm, 400mm, 500mm, and 600mm telephoto lenses.

Wide-angle and Ultrawide-angle Lenses

Wide-angle lenses, as the name implies, provide a very wide angle of view of the scene you're photographing. Wide-angle lenses are great for photographing a variety of subjects, but they're really excellent for subjects such as landscapes and group portraits where you need to capture a wide area of view.

The focal-length range of wide-angle lenses starts out at about 10mm (ultrawide) and extends to about 24mm (wide angle). Most wide-angle lenses on the market today are zoom lenses, although there are quite a few prime lenses available. Wide-angle lenses arc generally *rectilinear*, meaning that there are lens elements built in to the lens to correct the distortion that's common with wide-angle lenses; this way, the lines near the edges of the frame appear straight. Fisheye lenses, which are also a type of wide-angle lens, are *curvilinear*; the lens elements aren't corrected, resulting in severe optical distortion. I discuss fisheye lenses later in this chapter.

In recent years, lens technology has grown rapidly, making high-quality ultrawide-angle lenses affordable. In the past, ultrawide-angle lenses were rare, prohibitively expensive, and out of reach for most amateur photographers. These days, it's very easy to find a relatively inexpensive ultrawide-angle lens. Most wide-angle zoom lenses run the gamut from ultrawide to wide angle. Some of the ones that work with the D3000 include the following:

Image courtesy of Nikon, Inc.
5.5 Nikkor 10-24mm f/3.5-4.5

▶ **Nikkor 10-24mm f/3.5-4.5.** This is Nikon's newest ultrawide DX zoom. The 10-24mm was specifically designed for DX cameras. This lens gives you a very wide field of view, and it's small and well built with little distortion. The AF-S motor allows it to focus perfectly with the D3000.

▶ **Sigma 10-20mm f/4-5.6.** When it comes to third-party lenses, I prefer Sigma lenses. They have superior build quality and their Hyper-Sonic Motor (HSM), which is similar to Nikon's Silent Wave AF-S motor, allows this lens to autofocus with the D3000. This lens is a little less sharp than the Nikon and it has a reduced range on the long end, but it's much cheaper. You may not even miss the longer range at all, as it's most likely covered by one of your other lenses such as the 18-55mm kit lens. It's also slower than the offerings of most other manufacturers, but sometimes you must make concessions with your lens choices.

▶ **Tokina AT-X 124 AF Pro DX II.** This is a 12-24mm f/4 wide-angle lens. This is Tokina's updated version of the original 12-24mm f/4, which is a very sharp and relatively inexpensive lens. Be sure if you get this lens that you get the II version. The original version will not autofocus with the D3000.

Sigma also offers a 12-24mm lens. It's built like a tank and has an HSM motor. The Sigma is also useable with Nikon FX cameras, which may be something to consider if you're planning to upgrade to FX sometime in the future.

When to use a wide-angle lens

You can use wide-angle lenses for a broad variety of subjects, and they're great for creating dynamic images with interesting results. Once you get used to seeing the world through a wide-angle lens, you may find that your images start to be more creative, and you may look at your subjects differently. There are many considerations when you use a wide-angle lens. Here are a few:

▶ **More depth of field.** Wide-angle lenses allow you to get more of the scene in focus than you can when you use a midrange or telephoto lens at the same aperture and distance from the subject.

▶ **Wider field of view.** Wide-angle lenses allow you to fit more of your subject into your images. The shorter the focal length, the more you can fit in. This can be especially beneficial when you shoot landscape photos where you want to fit an immense scene into your photo.

▶ **Perspective distortion.** Using wide-angle lenses causes things that are closer to the lens to look disproportionately larger than things that are farther away. You can use perspective distortion to your advantage to emphasize objects in the foreground if you want the subject to stand out in the frame.

▶ **Handholding.** At shorter focal lengths, it's possible to hold the camera steadier than you can at longer focal lengths. At 14mm, it's entirely possible to handhold your camera at 1/15 second without worrying about camera shake.

▶ **Environmental portraits.** Although using a wide-angle lens isn't the best choice for standard close-up portraits, wide-angle lenses work great for environmental portraits where you want to show a person in her surroundings.

Wide-angle lenses can also help pull you into a subject. With most wide-angle lenses, you can focus very close. This helps you get right up close and personal with the subject while creating the perspective distortion that wide-angle lenses are known for. Don't be afraid to get close to your subject to make a more dynamic image. The worst wide-angle images are the ones that have a tiny subject in the middle of an empty area.

Understanding limitations

Wide-angle lenses are very distinctive when it comes to the way they portray your images, and they also have some limitations that you may not find in lenses with longer focal lengths. There are also some pitfalls that you need to be aware of when using wide-angle lenses:

▶ **Soft corners.** The most common problem that wide-angle lenses, especially zooms, have is that they soften the images in the corners. This is most prevalent at wide apertures, such as f/2.8 and f/4, and the corners usually sharpen up by f/8 (depending on the lens). This problem is greatest in lower-priced lenses.

▶ **Vignetting.** This is the darkening of the corners in the image. This occurs because the light that's needed to capture such a wide angle of view must come from an oblique angle. When the light comes in at such an angle, the aperture is effectively smaller. The aperture opening no longer appears as a circle but is shaped like a cat's eye. Stopping down the aperture 1 to 2 stops reduces this effect, and stopping down by 3 stops usually eliminates any vignetting.

▶ **Perspective distortion.** Perspective distortion is a double-edged sword: It can make your images look very interesting or make them look terrible. One of the reasons that a wide-angle lens isn't recommended for close-up portraits is that it distorts the face, making the nose look too big and the ears too small. This can make for a very unflattering portrait.

▶ **Barrel distortion.** Wide-angle lenses, even rectilinear lenses, are often plagued with this specific type of distortion, which causes straight lines outside the image center to appear to bend outward (similar to a barrel). This can be unwanted when doing architectural photography. Fortunately, Adobe Photoshop and other image-editing software allow you to fix this problem relatively easily.

5.6 A shot taken with a wide-angle lens can add an interesting perspective to some images.

Standard or Midrange Lenses

Standard, or midrange, zoom lenses fall in the middle of the focal-length scale. Zoom lenses of this type usually start at a moderately wide angle of around 16–18mm and zoom in to a short telephoto range. These lenses work great for most general photography applications and can be used successfully for everything from architectural to portrait photography. Basically, this type of lens covers the most useful focal lengths and will probably spend the most time on your camera. The 18-55mm kit lens falls into this range.

Here are some of the options for midrange lenses:

▶ **Nikkor 17-55mm f/2.8.** This is Nikon's top-of-the-line standard DX zoom lens. It's a professional lens that has a fast aperture of f/2.8 over the whole zoom range and is extremely sharp at all focal lengths and apertures. The build quality on this lens is excellent, as most of Nikon's pro lenses are. The 17-55mm has Nikon's super-quiet and fast-focusing Silent Wave Motor as well as ED glass elements to reduce chromatic aberration. This lens is top-notch all around and is worth every penny of the price tag.

Image courtesy of Nikon, Inc.
5.7 Nikkor 17-55mm f/2.8

▶ **Sigma 17-35mm f/2.8-4.** This lens is a low-cost alternative to the Nikon 17-55mm that has a variable aperture of f/2.8 on the wide end and f/4 on the long end. You can get this lens for about one-quarter of the cost of the Nikon 17-55mm and it's much smaller and lighter. It's got Sigma's HSM so it can auto-focus with the D3000. It's a great walking-around lens for standard shots. This lens also works with FX cameras for future compatibility.

There are a few prime lenses that fit into this category: the 28mm, 30mm, and 35mm. These lenses are considered "normal" lenses for DX cameras in that they approximate the normal field of view of the human eye. They are great all-around lenses. They come with apertures of f/2.8 or faster and can be found for less than $400, with the exception of the rare Nikon 28mm f/1.4, which can run up to $5,000 in new condition (if you can find it). There are only a couple of normal prime lenses available at this time that can autofocus with the D3000: the Nikon 35mm f/1.8G and the Sigma 30mm f/1.4 HSM. Both are great lenses, but at right around $200, you can't go wrong with the Nikon. This is the lens that I use most with all DX cameras, including the D3000.

Telephoto Lenses

Telephoto lenses have very long focal lengths and are used to get closer to distant subjects. They provide a very narrow field of view and are handy when you're trying to focus on the details of a subject. Telephoto lenses produce a much shallower depth of field than wide-angle and midrange lenses, and you can use them effectively to blur background details to isolate a subject.

Telephoto lenses are commonly used for sports and wildlife photography. The shallow depth of field also makes them one of the top choices for photographing portraits.

As with wide-angle lenses, telephoto lenses also have their quirks, such as perspective distortion. As you may have guessed, telephoto perspective distortion is the opposite of the wide-angle variety. Because everything in the photo is so far away with a telephoto lens, the lens tends to compress the image. Compression causes the background to look too close to the foreground. Of course, you can use this effect creatively. For example, compression can flatten out the features of a model, resulting in a pleasing effect. Compression is another reason why photographers often use a telephoto lens for portrait photography.

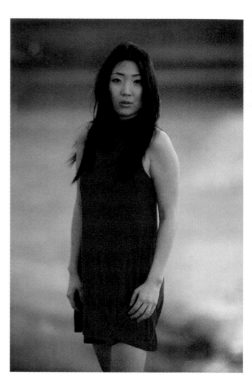

5.8 A 3/4-length portrait shot with a telephoto lens

A typical telephoto zoom lens usually has a range of about 55–200mm. If you want to zoom in close to a subject that's very far away, you may need an even longer lens. These super-telephoto lenses can act like telescopes, really bringing the subject in close. They range from about 300mm up to about 800mm. Almost all super-telephoto lenses are prime lenses, and they're very heavy, bulky, and expensive.

Super-Zooms

Most lens manufacturers, Nikon included, offer what's commonly termed a *super-zoom*, or sometimes called a *hyper-zoom*. Super-zooms are lenses that encompass a very wide focal length range, from wide angle to telephoto. The most popular of the super-zooms is the Nikon 18-200mm f/3.5-5.6 VR, shown here.

These lenses allow you to have a huge focal-length range that you can use in a wide variety of shooting situations without having to switch out lenses. This can come in handy if, for example, you are photographing a landscape scene by using a wide-angle setting, and lo and behold, Bigfoot appears on the horizon. You can quickly zoom in with the super-telephoto setting and get a good close-up shot without having to fumble around in your camera bag to grab a telephoto and switch out lenses, possibly causing you to miss the shot of a lifetime.

Of course, there's no free lunch, and these super-zooms come with a price (figuratively and literally). In order to achieve the great ranges in focal length, some concessions must be made with regard to image quality. These lenses are usually less sharp than lenses with a shorter zoom range and are more often plagued with optical distortions and chromatic aberration. Super-zooms often show pronounced barrel distortion (the bowing out of straight lines in the image) at the wide end and can have moderate to severe pincushion distortion (the bowing in of the straight lines in the image) at the long end of the range. Luckily, these types of distortions can be fixed in Adobe Photoshop or other image-editing software.

Another caveat to using these lenses is that they generally have appreciably smaller maximum apertures than zoom lenses with shorter ranges. This can be a problem, especially because larger apertures are generally needed at the long end to keep a high enough shutter speed to avoid blurring from camera shake when handholding. Of course, some manufacturers include some sort of Vibration Reduction feature to help control this problem.

Some popular super-zooms include the Nikon 18-200mm f/3.5-5.6 VR (mentioned earlier), the Sigma 18-200mm f/3.5-6.3 with Optical Stabilization, and the Tamron 18-270mm VC f/3.5-5.6. There are also a few super-zoom super-telephoto lenses, including the Nikon 80-400mm and the Sigma 50-500mm.

There are several telephoto prime lenses available. Most of them are pretty expensive, although you can sometimes find some older Nikon primes that are discontinued or used — and at decent prices. One of these lenses is the 300mm f/4. A couple of relatively inexpensive telephoto primes are in the shorter range of 50–85mm. The 50mm is considered a normal lens for FX format, but the DX format makes this lens a 75mm equivalent, landing it squarely in the short telephoto range for use with the D3000.

Nikon has recently released an AF-S version of the 50mm f/1.4. This is a G lens with the Silent Wave Motor. It's fast focusing and sharp.

Here are some of the most common telephoto lenses:

▶ **Nikkor 70-200mm f/2.8 VR.** This is Nikon's top-of-the-line telephoto lens. The VR makes this lens useful when photographing far-off subjects handheld. This is a great lens for sports, portraits, and wildlife photography.

Image courtesy of Nikon, Inc.
5.9 Nikkor 70-200mm f/2.8 VR.

▶ **Nikkor 55-200mm f/4-5.6 VR.** This is one of Nikon's most affordable lenses and is actually a pretty strong performer for its price range. The 55-200mm VR is quite sharp and only has mild barrel distortion issues.

▶ **Nikkor 80-200mm f/2.8D AF-S.** This is a great, affordable alternative to the 70-200mm VR lens. This lens is sharp and has a fast, constant f/2.8 aperture.

▶ **Sigma 70-200mm f/2.8 HSM.** This is a good alternative to the Nikon lenses. The HSM motor allows for autofocus with the D3000 and the lens costs less than half the price of the Nikon 70-200 although you do lose VR.

Macro Lenses

A macro lens is a special-purpose lens used in macro and close-up photography. It allows you to have a closer focusing distance than regular lenses, which in turn allows you to get more magnification of your subject, revealing small details that would otherwise be lost. True macro lenses offer a magnification ratio of 1:1; that is, the image projected onto the sensor through the lens is the exact same size as the actual object being photographed. Some lower-priced macro lenses offer a 1:2 or even a 1:4 magnification ratio, which is one-half to one-quarter of the size of the original object. Although lens manufacturers refer to these lenses as macro, strictly speaking, they are not.

One major concern with a macro lens is the depth of field. When focusing at such a close distance, the depth of field becomes very shallow; it's often advisable to use a small aperture to maximize your depth of field and ensure everything is in focus. Of course, as with any downside, there's an upside: You can also use the shallow depth of field creatively. For example, you can use it to isolate a detail in a subject.

Macro lenses come in a variety of focal lengths, and the most common is 60mm. Some macro lenses have substantially longer focal lengths, which allow more distance between the lens and the subject. This comes in handy when the subject needs to be lit with an additional light source. A lens that's very close to the subject while focusing can get in the way of the light source, casting a shadow.

When buying a macro lens, you should consider a few things: How often are you going to use the lens? Can you use it for other purposes? Do you need AF? Because newer dedicated macro lenses can be pricey, you may want to consider some cheaper alternatives.

The first thing you should know is that it's not absolutely necessary to have an AF lens. When shooting very close up, the depth of focus is very small, so all you need to do is move slightly closer or farther away to achieve focus. This makes an AF lens a bit unnecessary. You can find plenty of older Nikon manual focus (MF) macro lenses that are very inexpensive, and the lens quality and sharpness are still superb.

 Some other manufacturers also make good-quality MF macro lenses. I have a
NOTE 50mm f/4 Macro-Takumar made for early Pentax screw-mount camera bodies. I bought this lens for next to nothing, and I found an inexpensive adapter that allows it to fit the Nikon F-mount. The great thing about this lens is that it's super-sharp and allows me to focus close enough to get a 4:1 magnification ratio, which is 4X life size.

Nikon currently offers two focal-length macro lenses under the Micro-Nikkor designation that autofocus with the D3000:

▶ **Nikkor 60mm f/2.8.** Nikon offers two versions of this lens — one with a standard AF drive and one with an AF-S version with the Silent Wave Motor. The AF-S version also has the new Nano Crystal Coat lens coating to help eliminate ghosting and flare.

▶ **Nikkor 105mm f/2.8 VR.** This is a great lens that not only allows you to focus extremely close but also enables you to back off and still get a good close-up shot. This lens is equipped with VR. This can be invaluable with macro photography because it allows you to handhold at slower shutter speeds — a necessity when stopping down to maintain a good depth of field. This lens can also double as a very impressive portrait lens. This is currently the favored lens in my arsenal.

Image courtesy of Nikon, Inc.
5.10 Nikkor 105mm f/2.8G VR macro lens

A couple of third-party lenses that work well with the D3000 are

▶ **Tamron 90mm f/2.8.** This lens is highly regarded for its sharpness. It's also got a built-in motor so it will autofocus with the D3000. I initially bought this lens instead of the Nikon 105mm lens, but I quickly returned it. Although it's a good quality lens, I didn't like the fact that the front element of the lens moves in and out during focusing. This can cause the lens element to hit your subject if you're too close and not careful, possibly damaging the lens. Also,

5.11 A shot taken with a macro lens

unlike the offerings from Sigma and Nikon, Tamron's built-in focus motor is very loud and very slow.

▶ **Sigma 150mm f/2.8 HSM.** This is another highly regarded lens for its sharpness. Fast, quiet focusing with the HSM. It's a great lens.

Fisheye Lenses

Fisheye lenses are ultrawide-angle lenses that aren't corrected for distortion like standard rectilinear wide-angle lenses. These lenses are known as *curvilinear*, meaning that straight lines in your image, especially near the edge of the frame, are curved. Fisheye lenses have extreme barrel distortion, but that's what makes them fisheye lenses.

Fisheye lenses cover a full 180-degree area, allowing you to see everything that's immediately to the left and right of you in the frame. Special care has to be taken so that you don't get your feet in the frame, as so often happens when you use a lens with a field of view this extreme.

5.12 An image taken with a Nikon 10.5mm fisheye lens. Notice how the lens distorts the horizon line.

Fisheye lenses aren't made for everyday shooting, but with their extreme perspective distortion, you can achieve interesting, and sometimes wacky, results. You can also "de-fish" or correct for the extreme fisheye by using image-editing software, such as Adobe Photoshop, Nikon's Capture NX or NX2, and DxO Optics. The end result of correcting your image is that you get a reduced field of view. This is akin to using a rectilinear wide-angle lens.

Using Vibration Reduction Lenses

Nikon has an impressive list of lenses that offer Vibration Reduction (VR). This technology is used to combat image blur caused by camera shake, especially when you handhold the camera at long focal lengths. The VR function works by detecting the motion of the lens and shifting the internal lens elements. This allows you to shoot up to 3 stops slower than you would normally.

If you're an experienced photographer, you probably know this rule of thumb: To get a reasonably sharp photo when handholding the camera, you should use a shutter speed that corresponds to the reciprocal of the lens's focal length. In simpler terms, when shooting at a 200mm zoom setting, your shutter speed should be at least 1/200 second. When shooting with a wider setting, such as 28mm, you can safely handhold at around 1/30 second. Of course, this is just a guideline; some people are naturally steadier than others and can get sharp shots at slower speeds. With the VR enabled, you should be able to get a reasonably sharp image at a 200mm setting with a shutter speed of around 1/30 second.

Although the VR feature is good for providing some extra latitude when you're shooting with low light, it's not made to replace a fast shutter speed. To get a good, sharp photo when shooting action, you need to have a fast shutter speed to freeze the action. No matter how good the VR is, nothing can freeze a moving subject but a fast shutter speed.

Another thing to consider with the VR feature is that the lens's motion sensor may overcompensate when you're panning, causing the image to actually be blurrier. So, in situations where you need to pan with the subject, you may need to switch off the VR. The VR function also slows down the AF a bit, so when catching the action is very important, you may want to keep this in mind. However, Nikon's newest lenses have been updated with VR II, which Nikon claims can tell the difference between panning motion and regular side-to-side camera movement.

While VR is a great advancement in lens technology, few things can replace a good exposure and a solid monopod or tripod for a sharp image.

Third-party Lenses

Several companies make lenses that
work flawlessly with Nikon cameras.
In the past, third-party lenses had a
bad reputation of being, at best, cheap
knock-offs of the original manufacturers. This is not the case anymore, as a
lot of third-party lens manufacturers
have stepped up to the plate and
started releasing lenses that rival
some of the originals (usually at half
the price).

Although you can't beat Nikon's professional lenses, there are many
excellent third-party lens choices available to you. The three most prominent
third-party lens manufacturers are
Sigma, Tokina, and Tamron. Each of
these companies makes lenses that
cover the entire zoom range.

5.13 Sigma 12-24mm f/4-5.6

CHAPTER 6

Working with Light

The most important factor in photography is light; without it, your camera is rendered useless. Whether the light is recorded to silver halide emulsion on a piece of film or to the CCD sensor on your D3000, you can't make a photograph without it.

Not only is light necessary to make an exposure, but it also has different qualities that can impact the outcome of your image. Light can be soft and diffuse, or it can be hard and directional. Light can also have an impact on the color of your images; different light sources emit light at different temperatures, which changes the color cast of the image.

The ability to control light is a crucial step toward being able to make images that look exactly how you want them to. In this chapter, I explain some of the different types of light and how to modify them to suit your needs.

Light, whether from a light bulb, the sun, or electronic flash, is required to make an exposure.

Natural Light

Though it is by far the easiest type of light to find, natural light is sometimes the most difficult to work with because it comes from the sun, is often unpredictable, and can change from minute to minute. A lot of times I hear people say, "Wow, it's such a nice, sunny day; what a perfect day to take pictures," but unfortunately this is not often the case. A bright day when the sun is high in the sky presents many obstacles.

First, you have serious contrast issues on a sun-drenched day. Oftentimes, the digital sensor doesn't have the latitude to capture the whole scene effectively. For example, it is nearly impossible to capture detail in the shadows of your subject while keeping the highlights from blowing out or going completely white.

Fortunately, if you want to use natural light, it isn't necessary to stand in direct sunlight at noon. You can get desirable lighting effects when working with natural light in many ways. Here are a few examples:

▶ **Use fill flash.** You can use the flash as a secondary light source (not as your main light) to fill in the shadows and reduce contrast.

▶ **Try window lighting.** Believe it or not, one of the best ways to use natural light is to go indoors. Seating your model next to a window provides a beautiful soft light that is very flattering. A lot of professional food photographers use window light. It can be used to light almost any subject softly and evenly.

▶ **Find some shade.** The shade of a tree or the overhang of an awning or porch can block the bright sunlight while still giving you plenty of diffuse light with which to light your subject.

6.1 A portrait shot using natural light from a window

▶ **Take advantage of the clouds.** A cloudy day softens the light, allowing you to take portraits outside without worrying about harsh shadows and too much contrast. Even if it's only partly cloudy, you can wait for a cloud to pass over the sun before taking your shot.

▶ **Use a modifier.** Use a reflector to reduce the shadows or a diffusion panel to block the direct sun from your subject.

D3000 Flash Basics

A flash is a device that electronically creates a quick burst of brilliant light by discharging a high voltage pulse of electricity through a tube filled with Xenon gas. This technology allows you to take photos in low-light situations by illuminating the subject for the brief duration that the camera's shutter is open.

Most camera manufacturers offer flash units; Nikon's are called Speedlights. Nikon Speedlights are dedicated flash units, meaning they are built specifically for use with the Nikon camera system and offer much more functionality than a nondedicated flash. A nondedicated flash is a flash made by a third-party manufacturer; the flashes usually don't offer fully automated flash features. There are, however, some non-Nikon flashes that use Nikon's i-TTL flash metering system. The i-TTL system allows the flash to operate automatically, usually resulting in a perfect exposure without your having to do any calculations. I'll cover the i-TTL mode later in the chapter.

 Not all Nikon Speedlights are fully compatible with dSLRs such as the D3000. **CAUTION** Speedlights such as the SB-900, SB-800, SB-600, and SB-400 can be used with full functionality, whereas older Speedlights such as the SB-80DX, the SB-50DX, the SB-28, SB-26, and SB-24 can only be used by manually setting the output.

Achieving proper exposures

If you are new to using an external Speedlight flash, exposure can seem confusing when you first attempt to use it. There are a lot of settings you need to know, and there are different formulas you can use to get the right exposure. Once you understand the numbers and where to plug them in, using the Speedlight is quite easy.

If you are using your Speedlight in the i-TTL mode, the calculations you would otherwise do manually are done for you, but it's always good to know how to achieve the same results if you don't have the technology to rely on and to understand how to work with the numbers. When you know these calculations, you can use any flash and get excellent results.

Three main components go into making a properly exposed flash photograph: Guide Number (GN), aperture, and distance. If one of these elements is changed, another one must be changed proportionally to keep the exposure consistent. The following sections cover each element and how to put them together.

Guide Number

The first component in the equation for determining proper flash exposure is the Guide Number (GN), which is a numeric value that represents the amount of light emitted by the flash. You can find the GN for your specific Speedlight in the owner's manual. The GN changes with the ISO sensitivity to which your camera is set; for example, the GN for a Speedlight at ISO 400 is greater than the GN for the same Speedlight when it's set to ISO 100 (because of the increased sensitivity of the sensor). The GN also differs depending on the zoom setting of the Speedlight. The owner's manual has a table that breaks down the GNs according to the flash output setting and the zoom range selected on the Speedlight.

 If you plan to do a lot of manual flash exposures, I suggest making a copy of the GN table from the owner's manual and keep it in your camera bag with the flash.

 If you have access to a flash meter, you can determine the GN of your Speedlight at any setting by placing the meter 10 feet away and firing the flash. Next, take the aperture reading from the flash meter and multiply by 10. This is the correct GN for your flash.

Aperture

The second component in the flash exposure equation is the aperture setting. As you already know, the wider the aperture, the more light that falls on the sensor. Using a wider aperture allows you to use a lower power setting on your flash, or if you're using the automatic i-TTL mode, the camera fires the flash using less power. This allows your flash to recycle (think recharge) faster as well as putting less of a drain on your batteries.

Distance

The third component in the flash exposure equation is the distance from the light source to the subject. The closer the light is to your subject, the more light falls on it. Conversely, the farther away the light source is, the less illumination your subject receives. This is important because if you set your Speedlight to a certain output, you can still achieve a proper exposure by moving the Speedlight closer or farther away as needed.

GN / Distance = Aperture

Here's where the GN, aperture, and distance all come together. The basic formula allows you to take the GN and divide it by the distance to determine the aperture at which you need to shoot. You can change this equation to find out what you want to know specifically:

▶ **GN / D = A.** If you know the GN of the flash and the distance of the flash from the subject, you can determine the aperture to use to achieve the proper exposure.

▶ **GN / A = D.** If you know the aperture you want to use and the GN of the flash, you can determine the distance to place your flash from the subject.

▶ **A × D = GN.** If you already have the right exposure, you can take your aperture setting and multiply it by the distance of the flash from the subject to determine the approximate GN of the flash.

Flash exposure modes

Flashes have different modes that determine how they receive the information on how to set the exposure. Be aware that, depending on the Speedlight or flash you are using, some flash modes may not be available.

i-TTL

The D3000 determines the proper flash exposure automatically by using Nikon's proprietary i-TTL system. The camera gets most of the metering information from monitor preflashes emitted from the Speedlight. These preflashes are emitted almost simultaneously with the main flash so it looks as if the flash has only fired once. The camera also uses data from the lens, such as distance information and f-stop values, to help determine the proper flash exposure.

Additionally, two separate types of i-TTL flash metering are available for the D3000: Standard i-TTL flash and i-TTL Balanced Fill-Flash (BL). With Standard i-TTL flash, the camera determines the exposure for the subject only, and does not take the background lighting into account. With i-TTL BL mode, the camera attempts to balance the light from the flash with the ambient light to produce a more natural-looking image.

When using the built-in flash on the D3000, the default mode is the i-TTL BL mode. To switch the flash to Standard i-TTL, the camera must be switched to Spot metering.

The Standard i-TTL and i-TTL BL flash modes are available with Nikon's current Speedlight lineup, including the SB-900, SB-800, SB-600, SB-400, and the R1C1 Macro flash kit.

Manual

When you set your Speedlight (either the built-in or accessory flash) to full Manual mode, you must adjust the settings yourself. The best way to figure out the settings is by using a handheld flash meter or by using the GN/D = A formula discussed previously.

 If you'd like detailed information on using Nikon Speedlights, you can check out the *Nikon Creative Lighting System Digital Field Guide, 2nd Edition* (Wiley, 2010).

Flash sync modes

Flash sync modes control how the flash operates in conjunction with your D3000. These modes work with both the built-in Speedlight and accessory Speedlights, such as the SB-900, SB-800, SB-600, and so on. These modes allow you to choose when the flash fires, either at the beginning of the exposure or at the end, and they also allow you to keep the shutter open for longer periods, enabling you to capture more ambient light in low-light situations.

Sync speed

Before getting into the different sync modes, you need to understand sync speed. The sync speed is the fastest shutter speed that can be used while achieving a full flash exposure. This means if you set your shutter speed at a speed faster than the rated sync speed of the camera, you don't get a full exposure and end up with a partially underexposed image. With the D3000, you can't actually set the shutter speed above the rated sync speed of 1/200 second when using a dedicated flash because the camera won't let you. This means you don't need to worry about having partially black images when using a Speedlight. But if you're considering using a studio strobe or a third-party flash, this is a concern you should consider.

Limited sync speeds exist because of the way shutters in modern cameras work. As you already know, the shutter controls the amount of time the light is allowed to reach the imaging sensor. All dSLR cameras have what is called a *focal plane shutter*. This term stems from the fact that the shutter is located directly in front of the focal plane, which is essentially in front of the sensor. The focal plane shutter has two shutter curtains that travel vertically in front of the sensor to control the time the light can enter through the lens. At slower shutter speeds, the front curtain covering the sensor moves away, exposing the sensor to light for a set amount of time. When the exposure has been made, the second curtain then moves in to block the light, thus ending the exposure.

To achieve a faster shutter speed, the second curtain of the shutter starts closing before the first curtain has exposed the sensor completely. This means the sensor is actually exposed by a slit that travels the length of the sensor. This allows your camera to have extremely fast shutter speeds, but limits the flash sync speed because the entire sensor must be exposed to the flash at once to achieve a full exposure.

Front-curtain sync

Front-curtain sync is the default sync mode for your camera whether you are using the built-in flash, one of Nikon's dedicated Speedlights, or a third-party accessory flash. With Front-curtain sync, the flash is fired as soon as the shutter's front curtain fully opens. This mode works well with most general flash applications.

One thing worth mentioning about Front-curtain sync is that although it works well when you're using relatively fast shutter speeds, when the shutter is slowed down (also known as dragging the shutter when doing flash photography), especially when you photograph moving subjects, your images have an unnatural-looking blur in front of them. Ambient light recording the moving subject creates this.

6.2 A shot using Front-curtain sync with a shutter speed of 1 second. Notice that the flash freezes the hand during the beginning of the exposure and the trail caused by the ambient exposure appears in the front, causing the hand to look like it's moving backward.

Red-eye reduction

We've all seen red-eye in a picture at one time or another — that unholy red glare emanating from the subject's eyes that is caused by light reflecting off the retina. Fortunately, the D3000 offers a Red-Eye Reduction flash mode. When this mode is activated, the camera turns on the AF-assist illuminator (when using the built-in flash) or fires some pre-flashes (when using an accessory Speedlight), which cause the pupils of the subject's eyes to contract. This stops the light from the flash from reflecting off of the retina and reduces or eliminates the red-eye effect. This mode is useful when taking portraits or snapshots of people or pets when there is little light available.

Slow sync

Sometimes when using a flash at night, especially when the background is very dark, the subject is lit but appears to be in a black hole. Slow Sync mode helps take care of this problem. In Slow Sync mode, the camera allows you to set a longer shutter speed (up to 30 seconds) to capture the ambient light of the background. Your subject and the background are lit, so you can achieve a more natural-looking photograph.

6.3 An image taken using straight flash at night. Notice how the subject appears to be in a "black hole."

When doing flash photography at slow speeds, your camera is actually recording two exposures: the flash exposure and the ambient light. When you use a fast shutter speed, the ambient light usually isn't bright enough to have an effect on the image. When you slow down the shutter speed substantially, it allows the ambient light to be recorded to the sensor, causing what is known as *ghosting*. Ghosting is a partial exposure that is usually fairly transparent-looking on the image.

When using Front-curtain sync, ghosting causes a trail to appear in front of
the subject because the flash freezes
the initial movement of the subject.
Because the subject is still moving,
the ambient light records it as a blur
that appears in front of the subject,
creating the illusion that it's moving
backward. To counteract this problem,
you can use a Rear-curtain sync setting, which I explain in the next section.

 Slow sync can be used in conjunction with Red-Eye
Reduction for night portraits.

 When using Slow sync, be sure
the subject stays still for the
whole exposure to avoid ghosting. Or
you can use ghosting creatively by purposely having the subject move to create a motion blur.

**6.4 An image taken using straight flash at
night and Slow sync. Notice how the
ambient light is balanced with the flash
resulting in a more natural look. Slight
ghosting results in reduction of sharpness.**

Rear-curtain sync

When using Rear-curtain sync, the camera fires the flash just before the rear curtain of
the shutter starts moving. This mode is useful when taking flash photographs of moving subjects. Rear-curtain sync allows you to more accurately portray the motion of
the subject by causing a motion blur trail behind the subject rather in front of it, as is
the case with Front-curtain sync. Rear-curtain sync is often used in conjunction with
Slow sync.

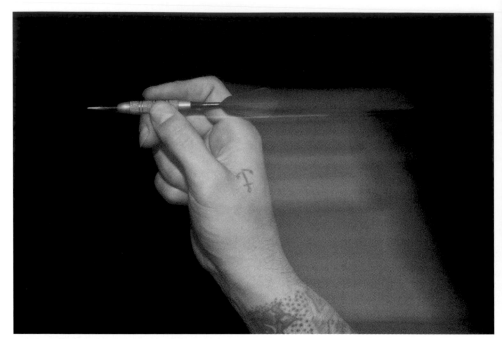

6.5 A picture taken using Rear-curtain sync. The flash freezes the motion at the end of the exposure, which causes the ghosting to appear behind the subject. This allows you to portray forward motion more accurately.

Flash Exposure Compensation

When you photograph subjects using flash, whether you use an external Speedlight or the built-in flash on your D3000, there may be times when the flash causes your principal subject to appear too light or too dark. This usually occurs in difficult lighting situations, especially when you use TTL metering. Your camera's meter can get fooled into thinking the subject needs more or less light than it actually does. This can happen when the background is very bright or very dark, or when the subject is off in the distance or very small in the frame.

Flash Exposure Compensation (FEC) allows you to manually adjust the flash output while still retaining TTL readings so your flash exposure is at least in the ballpark. With the D3000, you can vary the output of your built-in flash's TTL setting from –3 Exposure Value (EV) to +1 EV. This means if your flash exposure is too bright, you can adjust it down to 3 full stops under the original setting. Or if the image seems underexposed or too dark, you can adjust it to be brighter by 1 full stop. Additionally, the D3000 allows you to fine-tune how much exposure compensation is applied by letting you set the FEC incrementally in 1/3 stops of light.

Fill flash

Fill flash is a handy flash technique that allows you to use your Speedlight as a secondary light source to fill in the shadows rather than as the main light source, hence the term *fill flash*. Fill flash is used mainly in outdoor photography when the sun is very bright, creating deep shadows and bright highlights that result in an image with very high contrast and a wide tonal range. Using fill flash allows you to reduce the contrast of the image by filling in the dark shadows, thus allowing you to see more detail in the image.

You also may want to use fill flash when your subject is backlit (lit from behind). When the subject is backlit, the camera's meter takes into account the bright part of the image that is behind your subject. This results in a properly exposed background while

6.6 A picture taken without fill flash

your subject is underexposed and dark. However, if you use the spot meter to obtain the proper exposure on your subject, the background will be overexposed and blown out. The ideal thing is to use fill flash to provide an amount of light on your subject that is equal to the ambient light of the background. This brings sufficient detail to both the subject and the background, resulting in a properly and evenly exposed image.

All of Nikon's dSLR cameras offer i-TTL BL (Nikon calls this Balanced Fill-Flash) or, in laymen's terms, automatic fill flash, with both the built-in flash and the detachable Speedlights, the SB-900, SB-800, SB-600, and SB-400. When using a Speedlight, the camera automatically sets the flash to do fill flash (as long as you're not in Spot metering mode). This is a very handy feature because it allows you to concentrate on composition and not worry about your flash settings. If you decide that you don't want to use the i-TTL BL option, you can set the camera's metering mode to Spot metering, or if you are using an SB-900, SB-800, or SB-600, simply press the Speedlight's Mode button.

Of course, if you don't own an additional i-TTL dedicated Speedlight or you'd rather control your flash manually, you can still do fill flash. It's actually a pretty simple process that can vastly improve your images when you use it in the right situations.

To execute a manual fill flash, follow these steps:

1. **Use the camera's light meter to determine the proper exposure for the background or ambient light.** A typical exposure for a sunny day is 1/125 second at f/16 with an ISO of 100. Be sure not to set the shutter speed higher than the rated sync speed of 1/200.

2. **Determine the flash exposure.** Using the GN/D = A formula, find the setting that you need to properly expose the subject with the flash.

6.7 A picture taken with fill flash

3. **Reduce the flash output.** Reducing the flash output from your calculated exposure down 1/3 to 2/3 stops allows the flash exposure to be less noticeable while filling in the shadows or lighting your backlit subject. This makes your images look more natural, as if a flash didn't light them, which is the ultimate goal when attempting fill flash.

Diffusers

One of the easiest ways to improve your flash photography is to use a flash diffuser. These are simple devices that fit over or are placed in front of the flash head. As the name implies, a diffuser diffuses or softens the light. This helps to avoid that annoying dark black shadow that often appears next to your subject when taking photos using direct flash. There are a lot of different types of diffusers that range in price from $10 all the way up to $60. The type of diffuser I use depends on which flash I'm using. When using the built-in flash, I use a LumiQuest Soft Screen that I picked up at my local camera store for about $12. When using the SB-900 or SB-800, I use the diffus-ers that were included with them, and for the SB-600, I use a Sto-Fen Omni-Bounce. I've tried other diffusers, particularly the Gary Fong Lightsphere, and found it too bulky not to mention it's no better than the smaller diffusers that are easier to store in your camera bag.

6.8 A set of pictures — one without diffusion and one with diffusion. This shot was taken with the built-in flash.

I almost never use a flash or Speedlight without a diffuser unless I am specifically aim-ing for a scene that has very hard and directional light. If you use the built-in flash a lot, I recommend *always* using a diffuser. I cannot stress this point enough. It makes a huge difference in image quality.

Bounce flash

Another easy way to improve your flash pictures, especially snapshots, is to use bounce flash. Bounce flash is a technique in which you bounce the light from the flash unit off of the ceiling or a wall onto the subject to diffuse the light, resulting in a more evenly lit image. To do this, your flash must have a head that swivels and tilts. Most flashes made within the last ten years have this feature, but some may not.

When you attempt bounce flash, you want to get as much light from the flash onto your subject as you can. To do this, you need to first look at the placement of the subject and adjust the angle of the flash head appropriately. Consider the height of the ceiling or distance from the surface you intend to bounce the light from to the subject.

Unfortunately, not all ceilings are useful for bouncing flash. For example, the ceiling in my studio is corrugated metal with iron crossbeams. If I attempted to bounce flash from a ceiling like that, it would make little or no difference to the image because the light won't reflect evenly and will scatter in all directions. In a situation where the ceiling is not usable, you can position the subject next to a wall and swivel the flash head in the direction of the wall and bounce it from there. To bounce the flash at the correct angle, remember the angle of incidence equals the angle of reflection.

6.9 A picture taken with straight flash

6.10 A picture taken with bounced flash

You want to aim the flash head at such an angle that the flash isn't going to bounce in behind the subject so it is poorly lit. You want to be sure that the light is bounced so that it falls onto your subject. When the subject is very close to you, you need to have your flash head positioned at a more obtuse angle than when the subject is farther away. I recommend positioning the subject at least 10 feet away and setting the angle of the flash head at 45 degrees for a typical height ceiling of about 8 to 10 feet.

An important pitfall to be aware of when bouncing flash is that reflected light picks up and transmits the color of the surface from which it bounces. This means if you bounce light off a red surface, your subject will have a reddish tint to it. The best approach is to avoid bouncing light off of surfaces that are brightly colored, and stick with bouncing light from a neutral-colored surface. White surfaces tend to work the best because they reflect more light and don't add any color. Neutral gray surfaces also work well, although you can lose a little light due to lessened reflectivity and the darker color.

Unfortunately, you can't do bounce flash with the built-in flash on the D3000; you need an external Speedlight such as an SB-900, SB-800, SB-600, or SB-400.

Studio Strobes

One thing that bears mentioning is the use of studio strobes. Most professional photographers, especially those that shoot large sets and fashion, use studio strobes. These are large, high-powered flashes. They function in much the same way as a shoe-mount flash such as a Speedlight, but they run off of household AC and must be triggered by the camera using a sync cord or some sort of other trigger.

These strobes are completely manual, and the exposure setting must be figured out by using a flash meter or using the trusted GN / D = A equation.

There are two types of studio strobes: standard pack and monolights. Standard pack and head strobes have a separate power pack and flash heads that are controlled centrally from the power pack. Monolights are flash heads that have a power pack built in and you adjust them individually at each head. Monolights tend to be lower in power than standard strobes, but they are more portable and less expensive.

Nikon Creative Lighting System Basics

Nikon introduced the Creative Lighting System (CLS) in 2004. CLS is Nikon's name for their innovative flash technology that uses i-TTL metering and also allows the Speedlight to communicate with each other wirelessly. This allows you to position the Speedlights wherever you want and control the direction of light to make the subject appear exactly how you want. The Nikon CLS enables you to achieve creative lighting scenarios similar to what you would achieve with expensive and much larger studio strobes. You can do it wirelessly with the benefit of full i-TTL metering. To take advantage of the Nikon CLS, you need the D3000 and at least one SB-900, SB-800, or SU-800 as a commander and another SB-900, SB-800, or SB-600 Speedlight. With the CLS, there is no more mucking about with huge power packs and heavy strobe heads on heavy-duty stands, with cables and wires running all over the place.

The Nikon CLS is not a lighting system in and of itself but is comprised of many different pieces you can add to your system as you see fit (or your budget allows). The first and foremost piece of the equation is your camera.

Understanding the Creative Lighting System

The Nikon CLS is basically a communication system that allows the camera, the commander, and the remote units to share information regarding exposure.

A commander, which is also called a master, is the flash that controls external Speedlights. Remote units, which are sometimes referred to as slaves, are the external flash units the commander controls remotely. Communication between the commander and the remote units is accomplished by using pulse modulation. *Pulse modulation* is a term that means the commanding Speedlight fires rapid bursts of light in a specific order. The pulses of light are used to convey information to the remote group, which interprets the bursts of light as coded information.

Firing the commander tells the other Speedlights in the system when and at what power to fire. Using an SB-800 or SB-900 Speedlight or an SU-800 Commander as a master allows you to control three groups of remote flashes.

This is how CLS works in a nutshell:

1. **The commander unit sends out instructions to the remote groups to fire a series of monitor preflashes to determine the exposure level.** The camera's i-TTL metering sensor reads the preflashes from all the remote groups and also takes a reading of the ambient light.

2. **The camera tells the commander unit the proper exposure readings for each group of remote Speedlights.** When the shutter is released, the commander, via pulse modulation, relays the information to each group of remote Speedlights.

3. **The remote units fire at the output specified by the camera's i-TTL meter, and the shutter closes.**

All these calculations happen in a fraction of a second as soon as you press the Shutter Release button. It appears to the naked eye as if the flash just fires once. There is no waiting for the camera and the Speedlights to do the calculations.

Although you'll need to buy at least two Speedlights, one to act as a commander (SB-900, SB-800, or SU-800) and one to act as a remote (SB-900, SB-800, or SB-600), I'd highly recommend it if you're planning on doing any sort of advanced photography.

 For a definitive and in-depth look into the Nikon CLS, read the *Nikon Creative Lighting System Digital Field Guide, 2nd Edition* (Wiley, 2010).

Speedlights

Speedlights are Nikon's line of flashes. They are amazing accessories to add to your kit, and you can control most of them wirelessly. Currently, there are four shoe-mounted flashes that work with the D3000 — the SB-900, SB-800, SB-600, and SB-400. Two macro lighting ring flash setups — the R1 or R1C1 that include two SB-R200 Speedlights — are also available. You can also purchase SB-R200s for the R1 kits and the SU-800 Wireless Commander unit.

This is not meant to be a definitive guide to the Nikon Speedlight system, but a quick overview of some of the flashes Nikon has to offer and their major features.

 The SB-400 cannot be used as a wireless remote.

SB-900

The SB-900 Speedlight is Nikon's newest and most powerful Speedlight. This flash takes all the features of Nikon's previous flagship flash, the SB-800, and expands on them, adding more power, a greater range, and a more intuitive user interface. You can use the SB-900 as an on-camera flash, a commander flash that can control up to three groups of external Speedlights on four channels, or a remote flash that you control from another SB-900, SB-800, or an SU-800 Wireless Commander. The SB-900 automatically detects whether it's attached to an FX or DX-format camera, ensuring you get the maximum efficiency.

SB-800

The SB-800 has been recently discontinued, but if you can find one used it will work perfectly with the D3000. The SB-800 can be used not only as a flash but also as a commander to control up to three groups of external Speedlights on four channels. You can also set the SB-800 to work as a remote flash for off-camera applications. The SB-800 has a built-in AF-assist Illuminator to assist in achieving focus in low light. The SB-800 has a powerful GN of 184 at ISO 200.

SB-600

The SB-600 Speedlight is the SB-900 or SB-800's little brother. This flash has fewer features than its bigger siblings but has most of the features you need. You can use it on the camera as well as off-camera by setting it as a remote. Like the SB-900 and SB-800, the SB-600 also has a built-in AF-assist Illuminator. The SB-600 cannot, however, be used as a commander to control off-camera flash units. The SB-600 has an impressive GN of 138 at ISO 200, which, although it gives about 1 stop less light than the SB-800, is more than enough for most subjects.

 You can use a Nikon SC-28 TTL remote cord to get your Speedlight off camera. This is an economical way to start using off-camera flash without the need for an expensive Speedlight for a commander flash.

SB-400

The SB-400 is Nikon's entry-level Speedlight. It can only be used in the i-TTL/i-TTL BL mode. One nice feature is the horizontally tilting flash head that allows you to do bounce flash. Unfortunately, this only works when the camera is in the horizontal position, unless you bounce off a wall when holding the camera vertically. For such a small flash, the SB-400 has a decent GN of 98 at ISO 200.

 The SB-400 does not work wirelessly with the Nikon CLS. It only works when connected to the camera hot shoe or a Nikon SC-28 TTL remote cord.

SU-800 wireless Speedlight commander

The SU-800 is a wireless Speedlight commander that uses infrared technology to communicate wirelessly with off-camera Speedlights. It can control up to three groups of Speedlights on four different channels.

Continuous Lighting

Continuous lighting is just what it sounds like: a light source that is constant. It is by far the easiest type of lighting to work with. Unlike natural lighting, continuous lighting is consistent and predictable. Even when using a strobe with modeling lights, you sometimes have to estimate what the final lighting will look like. Continuous lighting is "what you see is what you get." You can see the actual effects the lighting has on your subjects, and can modify and change the lighting before you even press the Shutter Release button.

Continuous lights are an affordable alternative to using studio strobes. Because the light is constant and consistent, the learning curve is also less steep. With strobes, you need to experiment with the exposure or use a flash meter. With continuous lights, you can use the Matrix meter on the D3000 to yield excellent results.

As with other lighting systems, there are a lot of continuous light options. Here are a few of the more common ones:

▶ **Incandescent.** Incandescent, or tungsten, lights are the most common type of lights. Thomas Edison invented this type of light: Your typical light bulb is a tungsten lamp. With tungsten lamps, an electrical current runs through a tungsten filament, heating it and causing it to emit light. This type of continuous lighting is the source of the name "hot lights."

▶ **Halogen.** Halogen lights, which are much brighter than typical tungsten lights, are actually very similar. They are considered a type of incandescent light. Halogen lights also employ a tungsten filament, but include a halogen vapor in the gas inside the lamp. The color temperature of halogen lamps is higher than the color temperature of standard tungsten lamps.

▶ **Fluorescent.** Fluorescent lighting, which most of you are familiar with, is everywhere these days. It is in the majority of office buildings, stores, and even in your own house. In a fluorescent lamp, electrical energy changes a small amount of mercury into a gas. The electrons collide with the mercury gas atoms, causing them to release photons, which in turn cause the phosphor coating inside the lamp to glow. Because this reaction doesn't create much heat, fluorescent lamps are much cooler and more energy efficient than tungsten and halogen lamps. These lights are commonly used in lighting for TV shows.

Incandescent and halogen

Although incandescent and halogen lights make it easier to see what you're photographing and cost less, there are quite a few drawbacks to using these lights for serious photography work. First, they are hot. When a model has to sit under lamps for any length of time, he gets hot and starts to sweat. This is also a problem with food photography. It can cause your food to change consistency or even to sweat; for example, cheese that has been refrigerated. On the other hand, it can help keep hot food looking fresh and hot.

Second, although incandescent lights appear to be very bright to you and your subject, they actually produce less light than a standard flash unit. For example, a 200-watt tungsten light and a 200-watt-second strobe use the same amount of electricity per second, so they should be equally bright, right? Wrong. Because the flash discharges all 200 watts of energy in a fraction of a second, the flash is actually much, much brighter. Why does this matter? Because when you need a fast shutter speed or a small aperture, the strobe can give you more light in a shorter time. An SB-600 gives you about 30-watt-seconds of light at full power. To get an equivalent amount of light at the maximum sync speed of 1/200 second from a tungsten light, you would need a 7500-watt lamp! Of course, if your subject is static, you don't need to use a fast shutter speed; in this case, you can use one 30-watt light bulb for a 1-second exposure or a 60-watt lamp for a 1/2-second exposure.

Other disadvantages of using incandescent lights include:

- ▶ **Color temperature inconsistency.** The color temperature of the lamps changes as your household current varies and as the lamps get more and more use. The color temperature may be inconsistent from manufacturer to manufacturer and may even vary within the same types of bulbs.

- ▶ **Light modifiers are more expensive.** Because most continuous lights are hot, modifiers such as softboxes need to be made to withstand the heat; this makes them more expensive than the standard equipment intended to be used for strobes.

- ▶ **Short lamp life.** Incandescent lights tend to have a shorter life than flash tubes, so you'll have to replace them more often.

Although incandescent lights have quite a few disadvantages, they are by far the most affordable type of lights you can buy. Many photographers who are starting out use inexpensive work lights they can buy at any hardware store for less than $10. These lights use a standard light bulb and often have a reflector to direct the light; they also come with a clamp you can use to attach them to a stand or anything else you have handy that might be stable.

Halogen work lamps, also readily available at any hardware store, offer a higher light output than a standard light, generally speaking. The downside is they are very hot, and the larger lights can be a bit unwieldy. You also may have to come up with some creative ways to get the lights in the position you want them. Some halogen work lamps come complete with a tripod stand. If you can afford it, I'd recommend buying these; they're easier to set up and less of an aggravation in the long run. The single halogen work lamps that are usually designed to sit on a table or some other support are readily available for less than $20; the double halogen work lamps with two 500-watt lights and a 6-foot tripod stand are usually available for less than $40.

If you're really serious about lighting with hot lights, you may want to invest in a photographic hot-light kit. These kits are widely available from any photography or video store. They usually come with lights, light stands, and sometimes with light modifiers such as umbrellas or softboxes for diffusing the light for a softer look. The kits can be relatively inexpensive, with two lights, two stands, and two umbrellas for around $100. Or you can buy much more elaborate setups ranging in price up to $2,000. I've searched the Internet for these kits and have found the best deals are on eBay.

Fluorescent

Fluorescent lights have a lot of advantages over incandescent lights; they run at much lower temperatures and use much less electricity than standard incandescent lights. Fluorescent lights are also a much softer light source than incandescent lights.

In the past, fluorescent lights weren't considered viable for photographic applications because they cast a sickly green light on the subject. Today, most fluorescent lamps for use in photography are color corrected to match either daylight or incandescent lights. Also, given white balance is adjustable in the camera or in Photoshop with RAW files, using fluorescents has become much easier because you don't have to worry about color-correcting filters and special films.

These days, because more people are using fluorescent lights, light modifiers are more readily available. They allow you to control the light to make it softer or harder and directional or diffused.

Fluorescent light kits are readily available through most photography stores and online. These kits are a little more expensive than the incandescent light kits — an average kit with two light stands, reflectors, and bulbs costs about $160. Fluorescent kits aren't usually equipped with umbrellas or softboxes because the light is already fairly soft. You can buy these kinds of accessories and there are kits available that come with softboxes and umbrellas, although they cost significantly more.Unfortunately, there aren't many low-cost alternatives to buying a fluorescent light kit. The only real option is to use the clamp light mentioned earlier in the chapter and fit it with a fluorescent bulb that has a standard bulb base on it. These types of fluorescent bulbs are readily available at any store that sells light bulbs.

Light Modifiers

Light modifiers do exactly what their name says they do: They modify light. When you set up a photographic shot, in essence, you are building a scene using light. For some images, you may want a hard light that is very directional; for others, a soft, diffused light works better. Light modifiers allow you to control the light so you can direct it where you need it, give it the quality the image calls for, and even add color or texture to the image.

Umbrellas

The most common type of light modifier is the umbrella. Photographic umbrellas are coated with a material to maximize reflectivity. They are used to diffuse and soften the light emitted from the light source, whether it's continuous or strobe lighting. There are three types of umbrellas:

▶ **Standard.** This inexpensive type of umbrella has a black outside with the inside coated with a reflective material that is usually silver or gold in color. Standard umbrellas are designed so you point the light source into the umbrella and bounce the light onto the subject, resulting in a nondirectional soft light source.

▶ **Shoot-through.** Some umbrellas are manufactured out of a one-piece translucent silvery nylon that enables you to shoot through the umbrella like a softbox. You can also use shoot-through umbrellas to bounce the light, as previously mentioned.

▶ **Convertible.** This umbrella is similar to a shoot-through umbrella but it has a removable black cover on the outside. You can use convertible umbrellas to bounce light or as a shoot-through when you remove the outside covering.

Photographic umbrellas come in various sizes, usually ranging from 27 inches all the way up to about 12 feet. The size you use depends on the size of the subject and the degree of coverage you want. For standard headshots, portraits, and small to medium products, umbrellas ranging from 27 inches to about 40 inches supply plenty of coverage. For full-length portraits and larger products, a 60- to 72-inch umbrella is generally recommended. If you're photographing groups of people or especially large products, you'll need to go beyond the 72-inch umbrella.

The larger the umbrella is, the softer the light falling on the subject from the light source. It is also the case that the larger the umbrella is, the less light you have falling on your subject. Generally, the small to medium umbrellas lose about a stop and a half to 2 stops of light. Larger umbrellas generally lose 2 or more stops of light because the light is being spread out over a larger area.

Smaller umbrellas tend to have a much more directional light than larger umbrellas. With all umbrellas, the closer your umbrella is to the subject, the more diffuse the light is.

Choosing the right umbrella is a matter of personal preference. Features to keep in mind when choosing your umbrella include the type, size, and portability. You also want to consider how they work with your light source. For example, regular and convertible umbrellas return more light to the subject when light is bounced from them,

6.11 A Speedlight with a standard umbrella

which can be advantageous, especially if you are using a Speedlight, which has less power than a studio strobe. Also, the less energy the Speedlight has to output, the more battery power you save. On the other hand, shoot-through umbrellas lose more light through the back when bouncing, but they are generally more affordable than convertible umbrellas.

Softboxes

Softboxes, as with umbrellas, are used to diffuse and soften the light of a strobe or continuous light to create a more pleasing light source. Softboxes range in size from small 6-inch boxes that you mount directly onto the flash head, to large boxes that usually mount directly to a studio strobe.

The reason you may want to invest in a softbox rather than an umbrella for your studio is that it provides a more consistent and controllable light than an umbrella does. Softboxes are closed around the light source, thereby preventing unwanted light from bouncing back onto your subject. With the diffusion material, there is less of a chance of creating hotspots on your subject. A hotspot is an overly bright spot usually caused by bright or uneven lighting.

Softboxes are generally made for use with studio strobes and monolights, although special heat-resistant softboxes are made for use with hot lights. Softboxes attach to the light source with a device called a speedring. Speedrings are specific to the type of lights to which they are meant to attach. If you are using a standard hot-shoe flash as your light source, some companies, such as Chimera (www.chimeralighting.com), manufacture a type of speedring that mounts directly to the light stand and allows you to attach one or more Speedlights to the light stand, as well. You mount the speedring to the stand, attach the softbox to the speedring, attach the Speedlight with the flash head pointed into the softbox, and you're ready to go.

Softboxes are available in a multitude of shapes and sizes, ranging from squares and rectangles to ovals and octagons. Most photographers use the standard square or rectangular softboxes. However, some prefer to use oval or octagonal softboxes because they mimic umbrellas and give a more pleasing round shape to the catchlights in the subject's eyes. This is mostly a matter of personal preference. I usually use a medium-sized, rectangular softbox.

As with umbrellas, the size of the softbox you need depends on the subject you are photographing. You can take most softboxes apart and fold them up, and most of them come with a storage bag that you can use to transport them.

6.12 A softbox

Diffusion panels

A diffusion panel is basically a frame made out of PVC pipe with translucent nylon stretched over it. Diffusion panels function similarly to softboxes, but you have a little more control over the quality of the light.

You place the diffusion panel in front of the subject and then you place your light source behind the diffusion panel. You can move the light closer to the diffusion panel for more directional light or farther away for a softer, more even light. For a full-length portrait or a larger subject, you can place two or more lights behind the panel, achieving greater coverage with your lights.

You can use a diffusion panel as a reflector, bouncing the light from your light source on to the subject. You can purchase diffusion panels at most major camera stores at a fraction of the price of a good softbox. You can disassemble the PVC frame easily and pack it away into a small bag for storage or transport to and from location.

 If you feel crafty, you can make a diffusion panel from items easily found in your local hardware and fabric stores. Numerous sites on the Internet offer advice on how to construct one.

6.13 A diffusion panel

Reflectors

The reflector is possibly one of the most overlooked pieces of equipment that are available for your photographic arsenal. These gadgets do precisely what their name implies; they reflect light. You can use them to reflect light from the sun onto your subject to add a nice soft fill light or you can use them with a Speedlight to bounce flash onto your subject to soften the light when using it as a main or use it to fill as well.

You can buy a fold-up reflector from your local photography store or you can use any number of things as a reflector. The most common is using a piece of white foamcore (available at any art supply store). You can also use white poster board, or some folks even use the lids from a Styrofoam cooler.

I recommend buying a fold-up reflector. These are sturdier and last much longer than the alternatives listed earlier, which can easily get dirty, fold, tear, or break.

Professional reflector discs are available in a multitude of sizes from about 2 to 6 feet and are usually circular or rectangular in shape (circular is most common). They fold up to less than half their open size. I have a small 22-inch reflector that folds up to 9 inches and fits perfectly in my camera bag and is great for doing on-location portraits. This disc has a white side and a silver side for more reflectivity. You can also find them in a shiny gold color that adds a nice warmth to the subject.

Reflectors can also be used as a bouncing surface for your Speedlight. Just as with the ceiling or wall bounce, this will give you a more pleasing and diffuse light.

A 5-in-1 reflector disc is probably the single most versatile lighting modifier you can buy. A 5-in-1 reflector disc has five panels in one kit. The basic disc is a translucent material that can be used as a diffusion panel. The 5-in-1 kit comes with a cover that zips on over the top of the diffusion panel. The cover is reversible and each side is covered with a different material: opaque white for bouncing; reflective silver, which can be used to bounce flash or to reflect light from a constant light source such as the sun; reflective gold, which is used in the same way as the silver but adds warmth; and black, which is used to *flag* or block light from the subject.

6.14 A reflector being used to bounce flash. The reflector is being held by a Photoflex LiteDisc Holder.

Unless you have an assistant who comes with you on every shoot, I recommend buying a reflector holder to support your reflector. I use the Photoflex LiteDisc Holder. This is an accessory that attaches to a light stand and has clamps to hold the reflector in position. This enables you to place the reflector exactly where you need while keeping your hands free so that you can operate your camera.

CHAPTER 7

Real World Applications

This part of the book goes deeper into different types of photography and covers the settings that are used to capture specific scenarios. Although having a good eye helps, the key to capturing great images is to know which settings to use to achieve the desired results.

Some of things covered in the following sections include what shutter speeds to use, what metering modes work best for different situations, how to use the scene modes to your advantage as well as many other tips and techniques that I have learned and developed over the years.

Of course, in this limited space these sections aren't meant to be exhaustive and definitive, but they point you in the right direction.

Knowing which settings to use and how to work with light lets you get creative with your images.

Abstract Photography

For the most part, when you photograph something you are concerned with showing the subject clearly. When photographing a portrait, you try to represent the face or some revealing aspect of the person; when shooting a landscape, you try to show what's in the environment, be it trees, mountains, or a skyline. However, when shooting abstract photography, you are working with the idea of the subject, rather than an absolute subject. The subject is less important than the actual composition. When attempting abstract photography, you want to try to bring out the essence of what you're photographing.

There are no hard and fast rules to photography, and this is even truer in abstract photography. With this type of photography, you may be attempting to show the texture or color of something. What the actual object is isn't necessarily important.

An abstract photograph should give the viewer a different perspective of the subject than a normal photograph would. There are a few hardliners who say that if you can recognize the subject then it's not truly abstract. To that I say: Abstract photography (or any abstract art) can be broken down into two types — *objective* and *nonobjective*. Objective abstract art presents something that can be recognized, but it presents it in an unusual way. Nonobjective abstract art takes the subject and breaks it down to a base element such as lines, forms, colors, and texture. In figure 7.1 using an ultrawide 10-24mm lens set to 10mm and getting down low allowed me to create a seemingly endless sea of pennies out of this art installation. For this shot I used a small aperture of f/22 to ensure that the image had a very deep depth of field.

7.1 Looking at something from a different perspective can turn almost anything into an abstract image.

Inspiration

7.2 Look for leading lines and patterns to make interesting compositions.

Almost anything can be used to create an abstract photograph. It can be a close-up of the texture of tree bark or the skin of an orange. Look for objects with bright colors or interesting textures.

Many structures have interesting lines and shapes. Cars can have interesting lines. Keep an eye out for patterns. Patterns can be anywhere — on the side of a building or the surface of a rock. Evening shadows often create dynamic patterns with the added benefit of the rich colors of the sunset.

Abstract photography practice

7.3 Finding beauty in the obvious is what abstract photography is all about.

Table 7.1 Taking Abstract Pictures

Setup	**Practice Picture:** Figure 7.3 is a study of smoke from a burning stick of incense. The twisting and swirling of the smoke creates interesting patterns that work perfectly for abstract images.
	On Your Own: Abstract photo opportunities can exist in even the most mundane subjects; take a closer look at things to find some interesting aspects.
Lighting	**Practice Picture:** For this shot I used an SB-900 off-camera controlled by an SU-800 commander. The Speedlight was set up camera left and aimed away from the background perpendicular to the camera lens. I also used a snoot to direct the light at the smoke and to avoid any light from hitting the background or lens. The Speedlight mode was set to Manual and the output level was set to 1/4 power. The background was a piece of black poster board.
	On Your Own: Try to find ways to use the lighting to your advantage. Finding the delicate interplay between shadows and highlights can give your images the added dynamic you need. For abstract images you can take advantage of natural light or you can create elaborate lighting set-ups of your own. There are no rules in abstract photography.
Lens	**Practice Picture:** Micro-Nikkor 105mm f/2.8G VR.
	On Your Own: You can use any type of lens to make an abstract image. Using wide angles can add strange distortions, or use a macro lens to come in close and focus on a minute detail.
Camera Settings	**Practice Picture:** For this shot I chose the Manual exposure mode so that I had complete control over the exposure settings. For a low-key image such as this the camera's meter generally tends to want to add too much exposure in order to bring detail out in the dark areas. I wanted the shadow areas to go completely black to draw attention to the smoke. I bumped up the ISO to 500 to avoid having the Speedlight fire at full power for every shot.
	On Your Own: There are no hard and fast rules for which settings to use when shooting an abstract image because the subject matter can vary widely. It helps to know exactly how the meter determines exposure so you can adjust it for your specific needs.
Exposure	**Practice Picture:** ISO 400 at f/16 for 1/200 second. Because focusing on smoke is next to impossible, I chose a small aperture to ensure that all of the details were in focus from the front of the frame to the back.
	On Your Own: Your settings can vary widely depending on your subject matter and lighting. With a relatively still subject you can use longer shutter speeds; when your subject is moving, be sure to use a faster shutter speed to freeze any motion.
Accessories	I used a tripod to assure that I didn't get any blur from camera shake.

Abstract photography tips

▶ **Keep your eyes open.** Always be on the lookout for interesting patterns, repeating lines, or strange textures.

▶ **Don't be afraid to experiment.** Sometimes something as minor as changing the white balance setting can change the whole image. Sometimes the wrong setting may be the right one for the image.

Action and Sports Photography

Capturing action has been an aspiration of photographers since the inception of photography. Freezing a moment of time allows you to study the subject in motion. These types of photographs often bring you closer to an event or freeze the moment, allowing you to see the action in a way that's just not possible with the naked eye.

 Action photography can be done with any type of moving subject, from a pet running up the beach, to a child running around at the playground, to a professional basketball player slam-dunking the ball.

Although the relatively speedy frame rate of 3 fps of the D3000 comes in handy when shooting action and sports, probably the most essential skill for achieving great action shots is timing. To get a great shot, you need to get the peak of the action. In order to capture the action at its peak, it helps to be familiar with the sport. For example, when photographing a track event such as the 100-meter dash, you know that as the runners come off of the starting blocks, there will be strength and energy in their form. Of course, catching the winner crossing the finish line is also a great time for a shot.

The best way to get a feel for the sport you're photographing is quite simply to stand back and watch before you start shooting. Taking a few minutes to act as a spectator allows you to see the rhythm of the action.

Another big part of capturing a great action shot is being in the right place at the right time. While this sounds like luck, it's not. Take basketball, for example; it's quite easy to be in the right place at the right time. With basketball, you know exactly where the action is going to be 95 percent of the time: right at the goal. With other sports it's not always quite as easy, but as I mentioned previously, watching for a while can give you an idea of where most of the action will take place.

Probably the most important camera setting for photographing action is the shutter speed. The shutter speed determines how the movement is shown in your photograph. For the most part, a fast shutter speed is used when photographing action. A fast shutter speed allows you to freeze the motion of the subject. Freezing the motion lets you do things like getting a nice sharp image of an athlete in motion.

Using a fast shutter speed isn't the only way to capture great action shots. Using a slow shutter speed can sometimes be exactly what you need to bring out the movement in an action shot. For example, when shooting any type of motorsports, it's very common for a photographer to use a slow shutter speed in conjunction with panning to introduce some blurring into the image to illustrate movement.

If you're not familiar with panning, it is a technique in which you follow your subject along the same plane that it is traveling. Generally, you would pan horizontally, but you can also pan vertically, although this can be more difficult.

Panning reduces the relative speed of the subject in relation to the camera, thereby allowing you to freeze the motion of the subject more easily than if you held the camera still and snapped the shot while the subject moved through the frame.

7.4 Using a fast shutter speed to freeze the motion and catching the athlete at the peak of the action is essential.

Inspiration

I tend to gravitate toward the more exciting events when I'm out taking action shots. BMX, skateboarding, and Motocross are some of my favorite types of sports to photograph. You may find you favor more low-key action events, but regardless of what appeals to you, just keep your eyes open. Nearly everywhere you look there is some kind of action taking place.

To find action scenes to shoot you may want to start by scouting out the local parks and recreation areas. Nearly every city has a skatepark these days. Check your local newspapers for sporting events. Often the local skateboard shops and bike shops have contests. I try to take pictures of people having fun doing what they love to do.

Using flash when shooting sports isn't always necessary or advisable, but in some cases it can help to separate your subject from the background, especially if the background is busy, as in figure 7.5.

7.5 For this shot I used a Speedlight to separate the rider from the background making the rider "pop."

 Be sure to ask permission before shooting an athlete with any type of flash. The Speedlight can momentarily blind the athlete causing disastrous results.

Action and sports photography practice

7.6 It takes lightning-fast reflexes to catch the action when photographing any type of fast-moving sport.

Table 7.2 Taking Action and Sports Pictures

Setup	**Practice Picture:** For figure 7.5, I was photographing a professional bull riding competition in San Antonio, Texas. I snapped this shot just as the cowboy was thrown from the bull and was hitting the dirt.
	On Your Own: You don't need to photograph professional events to get great images. You can catch action shots at a Little League game that are just as good as shots taken at a major-league game.
Lighting	**Practice Picture:** Oftentimes, especially when shooting indoor sports, you will find that even when shooting with a fast lens the light will be low. The overhead lights of the venue provided the light for this shot.
	On Your Own: When photographing outside, a good rule of thumb is to keep the sun at your back. When photographing action indoors try to make the best of what light you have.
Lens	**Practice Picture:** Nikon 70-200mm f/2.8 zoomed to about 90mm.
	On Your Own: Often when photographing sports you will need a long lens to capture the action close up. For nonteam sports such as skateboarding and BMX, you can often use a wide-angle lens to add an interesting perspective to the scene. When photographing indoors or night sports a fast lens is almost a necessity.

continued

Table 7.2 Taking Action and Sports Pictures *(continued)*

Camera Settings	**Practice Picture:** I chose Shutter Priority so that I could be sure that the shutter speed was fast enough to freeze the motion of the bulls and cowboys. Although these animals weigh 2,000 pounds they are extremely fast moving. **On Your Own:** Controlling your shutter speed is the most important aspect in action photography, whether it's choosing a fast shutter speed to freeze motion or a slow one to add blur.
Exposure	**Practice Picture:** ISO 1600 at f/2.8 for 1/800 second. Even at f/2.8 to get a fast enough shutter speed to freeze the action I had to have the ISO cranked up to a high setting. **On Your Own:** First and foremost, be sure that you choose a shutter speed that is appropriate for the subject and the effect you're after.
Accessories	I used a monopod to minimize camera shake.

Action and sports photography tips

▶ **Practice panning.** Panning can be a difficult technique to master, but practice makes perfect. The more time you spend practicing this, the better you (and your images) will get.

▶ **Pay attention to your surroundings.** Often when concentrating on getting *the* shot, you can forget that there are things going on around you. When photographing sporting events, be sure to remember that there may be balls flying around or athletes on the move. It's better to miss a shot than to get hurt in the process of trying to get the shot.

▶ **Know the sport.** In order to be able to effectively capture a definitive shot, you need to be familiar with the sport, its rules, and the ebb and flow of the action. Being able to predict where the action will peak will get you better shots than hoping that you will luck into a shot.

Architectural Photography

Buildings and structures surround us, and many architects pour their hearts and souls into designing buildings that are interesting to the casual observer. This may be why architectural photography is so popular.

Despite the fact that buildings are such familiar, everyday sights, photographing them can be technically challenging and difficult — especially when you take pictures of large or extremely tall buildings. A number of problems can arise, the main one being *perspective distortion.* Perspective distortion is when the closest part of the subject appears irregularly large and the farthest part of the subject appears abnormally small. Think about standing at the bottom of a skyscraper and looking straight up to the top.

Professional architectural photographers have special cameras that allow them to correct for the distortion. Nikon makes perspective control lenses to help with this but the lenses are optimized for full-frame cameras and don't offer enough degree of correction on DX cameras to make it worth buying the lenses which start out at about $2,000. Basically, you have to either fix the image using software or work with the perspective distortion to make a dynamic and interesting image.

One of the easiest ways to combat perspective distortion is to get some distance between the structure and the camera. In figure 7.7, instead of getting up close to the building and using a wide-angle lens to fit the building in I moved way back and used a short telephoto setting of 80mm.

7.7 Distance lessens the impact of perspective distortion.

Copyright and Permission

In most places, you don't need permission to photograph a building as long as it's a place to which the public has free access. If you are on private property, you should definitely request permission to photograph before you start. If you are inside a building, it is generally a good idea to ask permission before photographing as well.

Due to recent tightening of security policies, a lot of photographers have been approached by security and/or police, so it's a good idea to check the local laws in the city where you are photographing to know what rights you have as a photographer.

For the most part, copyright laws allow photography of any building on "permanent public display." Although the architect of the structure may own the copyright of the design, it usually does not carry over to photographs of the building. There are exceptions to this, so again, check local laws, especially if you plan on selling your images.

Inspiration

Because buildings and architecture are all around us, there are limitless possibilities to shoot. Try looking for buildings with architectural features that you may enjoy, such as art deco, gothic, or modern. The building doesn't necessarily have to be in tip-top condition. Sometimes photographing a building in a state of disrepair can give you an excellent image.

You don't necessarily have to include the whole building in the picture. Sometimes focusing on a small feature or aspect of the structure, as I did in figure 7.8, is all you need to do.

7.8 Isolating the skylight of this building allowed me to use the lines and patterns to make a relatively abstract architectural shot.

Architectural photography practice

7.9 Using a wide-angle lens to exaggerate the lines and angles of the building adds an interesting effect to this shot.

Table 7.3 Taking Architectural Pictures

Setup	**Practice Picture:** For figure 7.9, I shot the ultramodern structure of Austin City Hall. **On Your Own:** There are buildings everywhere you look. You don't necessarily need to photograph a grandiose structure. I made an interesting architectural shot of the house where Elvis Presley was born, which is nothing more than a two room shack.
Lighting	**Practice Picture:** When shooting architectural images I often like to shoot at night to add some ambience and color to the scene. **On Your Own:** When photographing at night look for buildings that are lit up. The different lights and colors can make the shot more interesting. When photographing buildings during the day, try to keep the sun to your back. Avoid shooting into the sun, which means your building is backlit.
Lens	**Practice Picture:** Nikon 10-24mm f/3.5-4.5 set to 10mm. I used the widest setting on the lens to use perspective distortion to exaggerate the lines and angles of the building. **On Your Own:** Generally, a wide-angle lens is needed to photograph architecture, but backing away from a building and using a longer focal length will help you overcome any problems with perspective distortion.
Camera Settings	**Practice Picture:** For this shot I chose the Manual exposure mode so that I had complete control over the exposure settings. For a night image such as this the camera's meter generally tends to want to add too much exposure in order to bring detail out in the dark areas, which causes highlights to get blown out and the sky to be way too bright. **On Your Own:** Controlling your exposure allows you to get the exact effect that you're after. I recommend bracketing your exposure when doing shots like this.
Exposure	**Practice Picture:** ISO 200 at f/8 for 10 seconds. I chose a small aperture to ensure that all of the details were in focus from the front of the building to the back. The slow shutter speed isn't a concern because there are no moving aspects in the image other than the leaves that appear in the top left. **On Your Own:** Your shutter speeds can vary widely depending on the time of day. Generally you want to use a small aperture to ensure that you have a good sharp image from back to front.
Accessories	A tripod was absolutely necessary to achieve a sharp focus during the long exposure. An ML-L3 remote was also handy to release the shutter without vibrating the camera by pressing the Shutter Release button.

Architectural photography tips

▶ **Shoot from a distance.** When taking pictures of tall buildings and skyscrapers try not to take your photograph too close to the base of the building. The perspective distortion can make the structure look like it's falling over. Although, this effect can be utilized as a cool special effect.

▶ **Avoid backlighting.** If the building you are photographing is backlit you will lose detail in the structure and the background will appear too bright. Try to take your picture when the sun is shining on the part of the building you want to photograph.

▶ **Be aware of lens distortion.** Different lenses can introduce distortion. Wide-angle lenses often suffer from barrel distortion that can cause the straight lines of the structure that are near the edge of the frame to appear bowed out. Either avoid placing straight lines near the edge of the frame or be sure to correct for the distortion in post-processing.

Concert Photography

This type of photography can be the most difficult to deal with. The lighting is erratic at best and can throw your meter off resulting in over- or underexposed images. The performers are often moving around necessitating a fast shutter speed to freeze them but the light is low so the ISO needs to be cranked up in order to get a fast enough shutter speed. This represents all of the worst shooting conditions that you can encounter in photography rolled up into one!

Yes, this type of photography is challenging, but that's where the fun lies. Getting the quintessential shot of your favorite performer when the odds are against you is where the thrill of concert photography lies.

For the most part, with concert photography the lighting comes from the stage lights. If you're shooting at a larger venue or concert usually the stage lighting is wonderful and you can get amazing images using relatively low ISO settings. The stage lighting engineers are paid to make the performers look good and you're essentially piggy-backing off their expertise; of course, *you* are in charge of the composition. Unfortunately, when starting out you'll be in places with less-than-perfect lighting. You may need to crank up the ISO all the way to 3200 (Hi 1) when using the kit lens. However I don't recommend going above ISO 1600. For these situations, I have started using the Auto ISO feature. I know that sometimes I may need to use high ISO for some shots but not all of them. I didn't want to waste my time switching ISO settings all through the show, so I set the ISO sensitivity auto control to On / Maximum sensitivity 1600 / Minimum shutter speed 1/250. You can set the Auto ISO in the Shooting menu under the ISO sensitivity settings option. Using a minimum shutter speed of 1/250 allows me to hand-hold the camera and freeze the action of the band members so that they aren't blurry.

For concerts I almost exclusively use spot metering and set the exposure for the performer's face because I'm not usually concerned about the background. Often it's preferable to lose detail in the background because it brings out the subject of the image much better. I will occasionally switch to Matrix metering when shooting a

7.10 Spot metering on the performer allows you to get a good exposure on the subject while ignoring the background lighting.

daylight event, when I want to include some background details in the image, or if the lighting is constant, but for flashing and moving lights I recommend staying away from Matrix metering because the moving lights thoroughly confuse the metering system resulting in widely varying exposures.

Most of the time the lighting is fairly dim and you need to shoot with the widest aperture available, and setting the camera to aperture priority allows you to set the aperture and let the camera decide the shutter speed. Using a wide aperture also allows you to throw the background out of focus to get rid of distracting elements in the background.

Some photographers are staunchly against using flash at concerts, preferring to shoot with the available light, but in smaller venues sometimes the light just isn't enough to get a good exposure, and you have no choice but to use a bit of flash. Bouncing your flash and using a diffuser is your best bet in this situation.

For most national touring acts, using flash is strictly prohibited.

Because performers are usually in motion, even if it's just the motion of strumming a guitar, I always set the focus mode to Continuous AF (AF-C) with the AF-area mode set to Dynamic. This allows the camera to track the performer if he should happen to move in the frame.

This type of photography is ideally done with a fast lens of f/2.8 or better. This allows you to keep your ISO settings relatively low for the best image quality. Unfortunately, at this time there are few affordable options for fast lenses that allow the D3000 to AF. The one exception is the new Nikon 35mm f/1.8G. This is a good normal lens and will get you good shots as long as you're not too far away. A standard focal-length zoom lens is what I recommend for this type of

7.11 Capturing a great pose with perfect lighting is the key to getting a great concert shot.

photography, the Nikon 17-55mm f/2.8 being the preferred lens. The kit lens can be used, but you'll be pushing the limits of the ISO settings to get a fast enough shutter speed.

Inspiration

A good way to get started with concert photography is to find out when a favorite band or performer is playing and bring your camera. Smaller clubs are usually better places to take good close-up photos simply because you are more likely to have closer access to the performers. Most local bands, performers, and regional touring acts don't mind having their photos taken. You can also offer to e-mail the performers some images to use on their Web site. This is beneficial for both them and you, as lots of people will see your photos. I spent a lot of time honing my craft in smaller clubs and venues for lesser known bands before I had a good enough portfolio to show to the agency, which now gets me access to the national touring acts at the larger venues.

Unfortunately, most large touring acts don't allow dSLR cameras into the venue. There are exceptions, but this is generally the rule. You may be able to obtain a photo pass for larger events by offering your services to a local publication who will then contact the band's publicist to request a pass for you.

Concert photography practice

7.12 In dark venues it's sometimes necessary to use a Speedlight.

Table 7.4 Taking Concert Pictures

Setup	**Practice Picture:** Figure 7.12 is an example of a pretty common shot that you will find at most small venues with limited lighting capabilities. I offer this shot because it's fairly typical although I suggest using flash only in extreme circumstances. **On Your Own:** Starting out in concert photography you will likely run across very bad lighting. Overcoming the challenges is the key to getting good shots.
Lighting	**Practice Picture:** For this shot I was shooting at a venue with very low light. I couldn't get a good exposure with a fast f/1.8 lens even at Hi 1 (ISO 3200) so I had to use a Speedlight. I used an SB-800 and I used an SC-28 off-camera TTL cord to get the flash off-camera to avoid the straight flash. I held the flash in my left hand high over my head. I set the Speedlight to TTL and dialed the Flash Exposure Compensation down to at least -0.7 to avoid an overly flashed look and to allow some ambient light to shine through. **On Your Own:** Bouncing your flash, using a diffuser, and getting the flash off-camera are essential to making the lighting work. Straight on-camera flash isn't recommended, as it can look flat and obvious. You can also try using Slow sync to capture some ambient light.
Lens	**Practice Picture:** Nikon 17-55mm f/2.8 zoomed to 50mm. **On Your Own:** Using a fast lens allows you to capture all the available light. The more light you can get the less likelihood there will be of needing to use the flash.
Camera Settings	**Practice Picture:** I chose Manual exposure in this situation because I was using flash. I generally experiment using different shutter speeds to get different effects until I find a setting I'm happy with. The settings often depend on the band as well. For punk rock bands, I'll use a faster shutter speed; for moodier bands, I'll often drag the shutter (use a slow shutter speed) to add ambient light, sometimes introducing a ghosting effect. **On Your Own:** Experimentation is part of the process of shooting bands. Changing your settings, especially when using flash can have interesting results.
Exposure	**Practice Picture:** ISO 1600 at f/2.8 for 1/60 second. I had the ISO cranked and the aperture open so that my Speedlight wasn't firing full power to allow a fast recycle time so that I could fire off frames rather quickly if need be. **On Your Own:** Your settings can vary widely depending on your lighting. For the most part, you will find that you need to open up your aperture and use a relatively high ISO setting.
Accessories	I used a Nikon SC-28 off-camera TTL cord to get the Speedlight off-camera to avoid a straight-ahead flash look.

Concert photography tips

▶ **Experiment.** Don't be afraid to try different settings and long exposures. Slow Sync flash enables you to capture much of the ambient light while freezing the subject with the short, bright flash.

▶ **Call the venue before you go.** Be sure to call the venue to ensure that you are able to bring your camera in.

▶ **Bring earplugs.** Protect your hearing. After spending countless hours in clubs without hearing protection, my hearing is less than perfect. You don't want to lose your hearing. Trust me.

▶ **Take your Speedlight off of your camera.** If you're using one of the Nikon accessory flashes, such as the SB-800 or SB-600, invest in an off-camera through-the-lens (TTL) hot-shoe sync cord such as the Nikon SC-28 orSC-29 TTL cord. When you're down in the crowd, your Speedlight is very vulnerable. The shoe mount is not the sturdiest part of the flash. Not only is using the Speedlight off-camera safer, but you also gain more control of the light direction by holding it in your hand. This reinforces my suggestion to experiment — move the Speedlight around; hold it high; hold it low; or bounce it. This is digital, and it doesn't cost a thing to experiment.

Flower and Plant Photography

One of the great things about photographing plants and flowers, as opposed to other living things, is that you have almost unlimited control with them. If they are potted or cut, you can place them wherever you want, trim off any excess foliage, sit them under a hot lighting setup, and you never hear them complain.

Some other great things about photographing plants and flowers are the almost unlimited variety of colors and textures you can find them in. From reds and blues to purples and yellows, the color combinations are almost infinite. Plants and flowers are abundant, whether purchased or wild, so there is no shortage of subjects. Even in the dead of winter, you can find plants to take photos of. They don't have to be in bloom to have an interesting texture or tone. Sometimes the best images of trees are taken after they have shed all their foliage.

Flower and plant photography also offers a great way to show off your macro skills. Flowers especially seem to look great when photographed close-up.

Flowers and plants don't necessarily need elaborate lighting setups or special lenses. For figure 7.13, I placed this small rose clipping next to a window for a very soft lighting effect. I used a relatively inexpensive Tamron 17-50mm f/2.8 lens zoomed to 50mm. I opened the aperture to f/2.8 to give it a shallow depth of field and a soft ethereal appearance.

7.13 Window lighting is perfect for flowers.

Inspiration

Flowers and plants have been inspiration for artists down through the centuries. Many artists chose flowers and plants not only because of their beauty but also presumably because you don't have to pay them to model!

Many famous artists such as Van Gogh have found inspiration in the beauty of plants; some of Van Gogh's most treasured paintings are the Sunflowers, Irises, and the many paintings he did in Arles of the wheat fields and cypress trees.

It's not only painters who have derived inspiration from plants and flowers, but many many photographers down through the years have used plants and flowers as subjects. Edward Weston regularly photographed different succulents such as the agave cactus as well as many other plants, including fruits and vegetables. His image of the pepper shot in 1930 is one of his most famous works.

7.14 Flowers don't have to be in the wild to make a nice photograph.

Flower and plant photography practice

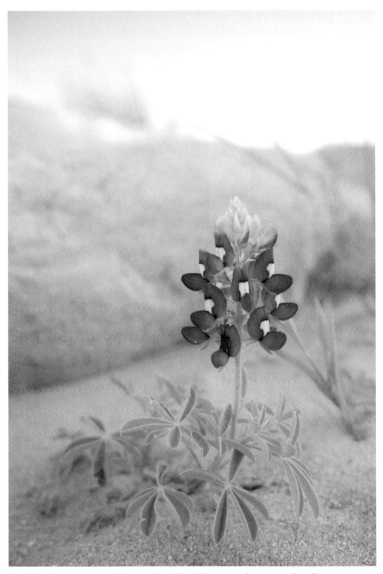

7.15 Unlike most subjects, backlighting works great for flowers.

Table 7.5 Taking Flower and Plant Pictures

Setup	**Practice Picture:** Figure 7.15 is a photo of a bluebonnet taken at the Pedernales Falls State Park.
	On Your Own: Parks and botanical gardens are a great place to find flowers and such. You can also pick up floral arrangements from your local florist.
Lighting	**Practice Picture:** This shot was lit by the late afternoon sun. Backlighting sometimes works pretty well on flowers. The translucent flower petals allow some light to shine through giving them a nice glow.
	On Your Own: For soft lighting bring your subject indoors near a window or find a subject in the shade. You can also wait for a cloudy day. In the bright sunlight use the contrast to your advantage. Keep an eye on your shadows and make sure that they work with the composition.
Lens	**Practice Picture:** Nikon 105mm f/2.8G VR. Although this is a macro lens, this technically isn't a macro shot. I used the length of lens to photograph a flower a little bit farther out.
	On Your Own: You can use any type of lens to take flower and plant shots. From wide angles to get a cool perspective to macro lenses to focus in on the details.
Camera Settings	**Practice Picture:** I chose Aperture Priority to control the depth of field. I wanted a slightly out-of-focus effect for the background while keeping the flower sharp. I used Matrix metering to get a good, even exposure.
	On Your Own: Controlling your aperture is key in focusing on the details in the image. You may want to use a wide aperture to blur unwanted elements from the background or a small aperture to be sure that the whole scene is in sharp focus.
Exposure	**Practice Picture:** ISO 100 at f/2.8 for 1/160 second. I used a wide aperture to blur the background to draw attention to the flower.
	On Your Own: Your settings can vary widely depending on your lighting. As I mentioned before, your aperture setting is important on controlling how much of the image is in focus.

Flower and plant photography tips

▶ **Shoot from different angles.** Shooting straight down on a flower seems like the obvious thing to do, but sometimes shooting from the side or even from below can add a compelling perspective to the image.

▶ **Try different backgrounds.** Photographing a flower with a dark background can give you an image with a completely different feel than photographing that same flower with a light background.

▶ **Try using complementary colors.** Adding different flowers with complementary colors to your composition can add a little interest to your image. Adding a splash of yellow into a primarily purple composition can make the image pop.

Landscape Photography

Landscape photography can incorporate any type of environment — desert scenes, mountains, lakes, forests, skylines, or just about any terrain. You can take landscape photos just about anywhere, and one nice thing about them is that you can return to the same spot, even as little as a couple of hours later, and the scene will look different according to the position of the sun and the quality of the light. You can also return to the same scene months later and find a completely different scene due to the change in seasons.

There are three distinct styles of landscape photography:

▶ **Representational.** This is a straight landscape; the "what you see is what you get" approach. This is not to say that this is a simple snapshot; it requires great attention to details such as composition, lighting, and weather.

▶ **Impressionistic.** With this type of landscape photo, the image looks less real due to filters or special photographic techniques such as long exposures. These techniques can give the image a mysterious or otherworldly quality.

▶ **Abstract.** With this type of landscape photo, the image may or may not resemble the actual subject. The compositional elements of shape and form are more important than an actual representation of the scene.

One of the most important parts of capturing a good landscape image is understanding *quality of light*. Simply defined, quality of light is the way the light interacts with the subject. There are many terms to define the various qualities of light, such as soft or diffused light, hard light, and so on, but for the purposes of landscape photography, the most important part is knowing how the light interacts with the landscape at certain times of day.

7.16 This an example of an abstract landscape image. I metered the scene to capture the eerie orange and red glowing sky of the sunset while allowing the land to fall into silhouette. The photo was taken at Enchanted Rock State Park near Fredericksburg, Texas.

Inspiration

For the most part, the best time to photograph a landscape is just after the sun rises and right before the sun sets. The sunlight at those times of day is refracted by the atmosphere and bounces off of low-lying clouds, resulting in a sunlight color that is different, and more pleasing to the eye, than it is at high noon. This time of day is often referred to as the *golden hour* by photographers due to the color and quality of the light at this time.

7.17 This is a representational landscape shot as the sun was starting to set giving the image a bit of a golden glow.

This isn't to say you can't take a good landscape photo at high noon; you absolutely can. Sometimes, especially when you're on vacation, you don't have a choice about when to take the photo, so by all means take one. If there is a particularly beautiful location that you have easy access to, spend some time and watch how the light reacts with the terrain.

Landscape photography practice

7.18 This is an impressionistic shot of Bull Creek in Austin, Texas.

Table 7.6 Taking Landscape Pictures

Setup	**Practice Picture:** Figure 7.18 is an example of an impressionistic land-scape image of Bull Creek in Austin, Texas. This is an infrared (IR) image, which gives the green foliage (which reflects a lot of IR light) a white glow, while the skies and water (which don't reflect IR) are dark. Infrared light is invisible to the naked eye. CCD sensors are sensitive to IR. IR light can have a detrimental effect on the standard images you create using visible light. For that reason Nikon installs an IR blocking filter in front of the sensor. Unfortunately, this means that IR photography with the D3000 can be quite difficult, but not impossible. **On Your Own:** Using unorthodox techniques can give your images a cool and/or surreal effect.
Lighting	**Practice Picture:** This was shot on a typical summer day with the bright sunlight overhead. **On Your Own:** Generally shooting landscapes using sidelighting when the sun is low yields the best results, but sometimes breaking rules can work in your favor.

Lens	**Practice Picture:** Nikon 35mm f/1.8G. I chose this normal lens because it has the same size filter threads as my IR filter. In order to capture an IR image, you first need to block visible light from reaching the sensor. An IR filter is used to do this. The most commonly used filter is the Hoya R72, which blocks out all wavelengths of visible light that fall below 720 nanometers (nm). The *nanometer* is the measurement used to determine the wavelength of light. The wavelengths of visible light fall between around 400 and 700nm, so at 720nm the light is just about beyond the reach of our eyes.
	On Your Own: A wide-angle lens is usually preferred for landscape photography. You can find a Hoya R72 filter in most common filter sizes. The smaller ones (52mm or 55mm are generally less expensive). Compose the shot with the filter off of the lens. After you compose the shot, you then must focus before placing the filter on the lens. Focusing can be a little tricky. Because IR light doesn't focus at the same point as visible light, you must make some adjustments. The best way to do this is to focus the camera, adjust the focus back just a little (turn the focus ring to the left), take a shot, and use the image review to check focus. If it's not in focus, continue to adjust focus. It's a bit of a trial-and-error process unless you're using and older Nikon lens that has in IR index mark.
Camera Settings	**Practice Picture:** I use the Manual exposure mode. When using one of the Auto exposure modes (P, S, or A), the camera's meter will underexpose, so using Manual exposure is necessary. I also set the Picture Control to Monochrome to preview what the image will look like in B&W. When shooting in color, preset your WB on green foliage such as grass or leaves.
	On Your Own: When shooting landscapes, it's generally advisable to set your aperture so Aperture Priority or Manual exposure is the best option.
Exposure	**Practice Picture:** ISO 100 at f/8 for 20 second. I chose a small aperture to ensure that all the details were in focus from the front of the frame to the back. Because the IR blocking filter on the sensor is very aggressive, a very slow shutter speed is needed to get a good exposure. I generally start my exposures at ISO 100 f/5.6 for 10 seconds and adjust the settings from there.
	On Your Own: Your aperture setting should be small to help ensure a nice sharp image.
Accessories	It's absolutely necessary to use a tripod when shooting IR, but a good tripod is something every landscape photographer should have.

Landscape photography tips

▶ **Bring a tripod.** When you're photographing landscapes, especially early in the morning or at sunset, the exposure time may be quite long. A tripod can help keep your landscapes in sharp focus.

▶ **Scout out locations.** Keep your eyes open; even when you're driving around you may see something interesting.

▶ **Be prepared.** If you're out hiking looking for landscape shots, don't forget to bring the essentials such as water and a couple of snacks. It's also a good idea to be familiar with the area you're in, or at the very least bring a map.

Macro Photography

Macro photography is one of the most popular and interesting types of photography out there. Sometimes you can take the most mundane object and give it a completely different perspective just by moving in close. Ordinary objects can become alien landscapes. Insects take on a new personality when you can see the strange details of their faces, especially their multifaceted eyes.

One of the most technically challenging aspects of macro photography is getting the enough of the subject in focus. The closer you are to the subject the less depth of field you get. For this reason, you usually want to use the smallest aperture you can (depending on the lighting situation). I say "usually" because a shallow depth of field can also be very useful in bringing attention to a specific detail.

Macro photography requires special lenses or filters to allow you to get closer to your subject. Most lens manufacturers offer lenses that are designed specifically for this purpose. These macro lenses give you a reproduction ratio of 1:1, which means that the image projected onto the sensor is exactly the same size as the physical subject. Some other lenses that can be used to do macro photography are actually telephoto lenses. Although you can't actually get close to the subject with a telephoto, the extra zoom gives you a close-up perspective. Telephoto lenses usually have a reproduction ratio of 1:4, or one-quarter size.

An inexpensive alternative to macro lenses are *close-up filters*. A close-up filter is like a magnifying glass for your lens. It screws onto the end of your lens and allows you to focus closer to your subject. There are a variety of magnifications, and they can be *stacked* or screwed together to increase the magnification even more. Although using close-up filters is an inexpensive way to get started, the image quality is going to be a little less sharp than when using a dedicated macro lens.

7.19 Using a wide aperture of f/3.2 to achieve a shallow depth of field draws attention to the details of this poppy seedpod.

Another relatively cheap way to get started in macro photography is by using a *reversing ring*. Reversing rings are adapters that have a lens mount on one side and filter threads on the other. The filter threads are screwed into the front of a normal lens like a filter, and you attach the lens mount to the camera body. The lens is then mounted to the camera backward. This allows you to closely focus on your subject. One thing to be careful of when using reversing rings is damaging the rear element of your lens; special care should be taken when using one of these.

Not all lenses work well with reversing rings. The best lenses to use are fixed focal-length lenses that have aperture rings for adjusting the f-stop. Zoom lenses simply do not work well, nor do lenses that have no manual aperture control (Nikon G lenses). You must also realize that when using one of these adapters you will have no autofocus capabilities nor will your camera's light meter function. You will have to choose all of your settings in Manual exposure mode.

Inspiration

7.20 This simple macro photograph of a coin literally only took minutes to set up.

There are many subjects you can choose from when doing macro photography. From insects to flowers to coins and stamps, almost anything can make an interesting macro shot.

One of the best things about macro photography is that you aren't limited to shooting in one type of location. You can do this type of photography indoors or out.

Macro photography practice

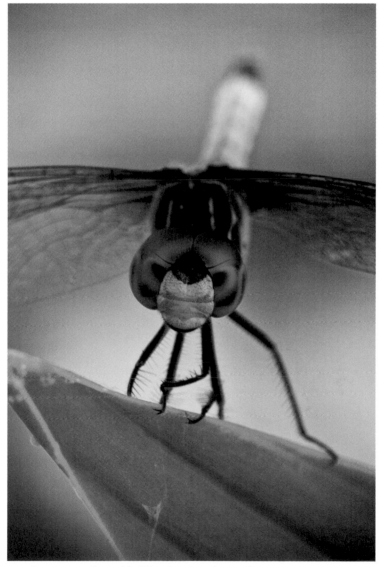

7.21 Insects such as this Blue Dasher dragonfly make interesting macro subjects.

Table 7.7 Taking Macro Pictures

Setup	**Practice Picture:** Figure 7.21 is an image of a Blue Dasher dragonfly that I captured at the Lower Colorado River that flows nearby my studio. **On Your Own:** Subjects for macro pictures abound even in the most mundane areas. Keep your eyes open for insects or objects with interesting textures.
Lighting	**Practice Picture:** This image was taken with available light although I probably could have added a little fill flash to really make the subject "pop." **On Your Own:** Often the easiest way is simply to use available light, but sometimes using a flash can make your images stand out. Getting an off-camera TTL cord for your flash and holding the flash right up next to your lens is an easy technique that works very well.
Lens	**Practice Picture:** Micro-Nikkor 105mm f/2.8G VR. This is Nikon's top macro lens. It's pretty expensive, but the image quality is unparalleled. **On Your Own:** Using a dedicated macro lens is the best option, but using close-up filters is a good option to start out.
Camera Settings	**Practice Picture:** I chose Aperture Priority to control the depth of field. I used Matrix metering to be sure that I got a good, even exposure of both the subject and the background. **On Your Own:** Controlling your aperture is key in focusing on the details in the image. You may want to use a wide aperture to blur unwanted elements from the background or a small aperture to be sure that the whole scene is in sharp focus.
Exposure	**Practice Picture:** ISO 800 at f/22 for 1/100 second. I chose a small aperture to get as deep of a depth of field as I could. You will notice that even at a very small aperture of f/22 when shooting this close up, depth of field is still very shallow allowing only the dragonfly's face and eyes to be in sharp focus. To allow me to set an aperture that small while still getting a relatively fast shutter speed to avoid blur from camera shake, I used an ISO setting of 800. The VR was turned on to help with stabilization. **On Your Own:** Focusing close up magnifies the effect of camera shake when handholding the camera. Oftentimes you will need to set your ISO rather high to be sure that you can get a fast shutter speed and a small aperture so that your images are razor sharp. Part of the appeal of Macro photographs are the sharpness of the minute details and a blurry image will ruin this.
Accessories	A ring flash is a great accessory for getting nice even lighting with macro shots. This type of flash attaches to the front of the lens for on-axis lighting. The Phoenix RF-46N is an inexpensive (about $129) unit that works using Nikon's iTTL flash metering.

Macro photography tips

▶ **Use a remote shutter release.** If using a tripod, using a remote shutter release can also help reduce blur from camera shake. The Nikon ML-L3 Wireless Remote Control is a very inexpensive option. You can also use the self-timer.

▶ **Use side lighting.** To bring out the texture of your subject, be sure that the subject is being lit from the side.

▶ **Try using a tripod.** Using a tripod is a very good idea when doing macro photography to combat camera shake. Of course, when photographing living creatures, it may be a hindrance.

Night and Low-Light Photography

When the sun goes down and the light gets low, a whole new world of photography opens up. You can capture many different aspects and portray the world in a different light, so to speak. Taking photographs in low light brings a whole different set of challenges that are not present when you take pictures during the day. The exposures become significantly longer, making it difficult to hand hold your camera and get sharp images. Your first instinct may be to use the flash to add light to the scene, but as soon as you do this, the image loses its nighttime charm.

Almost any type of photography can be accomplished in low light from landscapes to portraits. Each type of photography has slightly different techniques and accessories, but the goal is the same: to get enough light to make a good exposure and to capture the delicate interplay between light and dark.

Generally when doing this type of photography I use Manual exposure and I bracket my exposures. I do this for a couple of reasons. First, bracketing allows me to be sure that I get the exact exposure that I'm looking for, and if necessary I can combine elements of different exposures. For my base exposure, I set the metering mode to Matrix and look at the light meter in the viewfinder. I generally start my exposure settings where the meter says that it's 1 stop underexposed. I find that this is generally pretty close to the right exposure. I bracket five frames at 1-stop intervals from my base exposure. You can use smaller (1/3) or bracket more frames if you want more or less latitude in your exposures.

7.22 Brightly lit buildings make greats subjects for night photography.

When doing night photography such as this I generally use small apertures and slow shutter speeds. I use these settings mainly for a few different reasons. First of all the slow shutter speeds allow anything that might be moving in the scene to not register. For example, when photographing a city street scene using a shutter speed of 30 seconds a person walking through the scene wouldn't register as long as he keeps moving. This also allows you to capture streaks from any moving light sources such as a car or truck's headlights. I also like to use slow shutter speeds because most metropolitan cities are located near a river or lake and the reflection of the city in the water gets a glasslike appearance with the longer exposure.

I use small apertures for two specific reasons. The first is that smaller apertures require slower shutter speeds to make an exposure. Second, when using a small aperture, any points of light that are in the scene are rendered as starbursts, which creates a cool effect. This is due to the diffraction of the light from the aperture blades; the smaller the aperture, the more pronounced the points are.

A fast lens is a great tool to add to your kit if you're planning on shooting a lot of low-light images where you need to keep up a relatively fast shutter speed. The Nikon 35 mm f/1.8 is a great inexpensive fast lens.

Inspiration

7.23 Using a slow shutter speed and zooming during the exposure is a cool trick.

One of the easiest ways to do night photography is simply to grab a tripod and venture out into the night. Set up the camera on the tripod and shoot! The tripod stabilizes your camera so you don't have to worry about camera shake with long exposures. You can use the long exposures to create special effects like the streaks of lights from moving vehicles. One of my favorite things to do when I visit any city is to photograph the skyline at night. The multitudes of different colored lights make these pictures vibrant and interesting. Even though these are shot in the dark, there is actually plenty of light to be found. Cities take on a different and more interesting character when photographed at night.

One interesting trick that you can do when photographing lights at night is to use a slow shutter speed and zoom your lens out during the exposure. This very simple technique adds a pretty cool light trail effect to your image. For figure 7.20 I used an aperture of f/5.6 and a shutter speed of 1 second. One cool thing about this trick is that you don't need a tripod to do it.

It's best to get a nice sturdy tripod for this type of work. A ball head on the tripod is also great for quickly composing your images. If you find yourself without a tripod don't fret. The VR lens allows you to handhold the camera at slower shutter speeds while still getting relatively sharp images. You can also use wide-angle settings when shooting in low-light handheld. Wide-angle settings are easier to hand hold at longer shutter speeds without camera shake.

Night and low-light photography practice

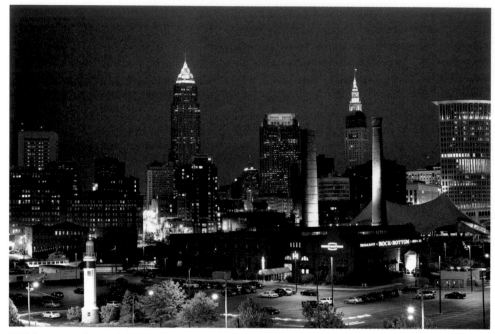

7.24 I try to take a night photograph of the skyline of every major city I visit.

Table 7.8 Taking Night and Low-light Pictures

Setup	**Practice Picture:** Figure 7.24 is a skyline shot of Cleveland, Ohio, taken at night.
	On Your Own: Skylines make great night photos. The combination of different colored lights gives you images with lots of saturated colors.
Lighting	**Practice Picture:** This photo was taken using available light.
	On Your Own: Generally, night photography is done using available light. Adding flash to the scene often kills the ambience of the image.
Lens	**Practice Picture:** 50mm f/1.4G
	On Your Own: You can use almost any type of lens to take night/low-light images. Faster lenses help you capture all the light that you can. VR lenses can also help in low light.

Camera Settings	**Practice Picture:** I set the exposure manually because I was bracketing as I usually do when shooting these types of images. I captured the image in RAW to be able to adjust the white balance in post-processing.
	On Your Own: Aperture priority works pretty well at night because you'll want to control your aperture setting either to open it up to get a faster shutter speed or to close it down to get a slow shutter speed. Shooting in RAW is a good idea because there are so many different light sources at night. You can adjust it to whatever looks good to you.
Exposure	**Practice Picture:** ISO 100 at f/8 for 20 seconds. I chose a small aperture to ensure that all the details were in focus from the front of the frame to the back.
	On Your Own: For shots like these, a slow shutter speed is generally used. It's not always necessary to use a high ISO setting especially when using a tripod, When handholding the camera a fast shutter speed is needed so a wide aperture and high ISO setting must be used.
Accessories	I used a tripod to achieve a sharp focus during the long exposure.

Fireworks

One of the questions I get asked most about low-light photography is how to photograph fireworks. Most folks seem to think catching these brilliant displays is a very difficult process but nothing could be further from the truth. Catching fireworks is a pretty simple and straightforward process.

The first thing you need to do is to set up your camera on a tripod. Without a tripod your fireworks images will be a blurry mess. Once you get your camera set up on a tripod, you're going to need to figure out where the fireworks are blooming and aim your camera lens in this direction.

Using a wide-angle lens is generally preferable to be sure that you get all the bloom in the shot. Using a telephoto lens can allow you to get some cool detail shots, but this is the exception rather than the norm.

Focusing should be done manually. Generally focusing the lens to infinity will work fine. Take a look at your images and adjust if necessary.

continued

continued

Use a low ISO setting and set your exposure manually. The aperture should be set to f/8 or f/11 and your shutter speed will need to be about as long as the fireworks explosion. The best way to control the shutter is to use the Bulb setting, which allows you to hold the shutter open as long as the Shutter Release button is pressed and held down. Alternatively, if you have an ML-L3 wireless remote shutter release, you can set the release mode to Quick Response Remote and set the shutter speed to the Time setting (this is the "bulb" setting when using the remote). This opens the shutter with a press and closes it with a second press. Using this accessory always makes sure you don't get blurry images from jiggling the camera while pressing the Shutter Release button. I recommend buying the ML-L3 as it's almost a necessity for this type of photography to be successful.

When the fireworks are launched open the shutter; when the bloom is over shut it. It's as simple as that. You may find you need to adjust your ISO and/or aperture setting a bit depending on the brightness of the fireworks as well as the amount of ambient light in the scene.

Night and low-light photography tips

▶ **Be patient.** Sometimes you will have to take many photos before you get one you like. It can be a trial-and-error process to find the exposure that works.

▶ **Show up early.** To get a good spot for shooting fireworks you may need to show up pretty early.

▶ **Turn on the VR.** The VR feature of your kit lens will help reduce vibration caused by handholding the lens at slower shutter speeds.

Portrait Photography

Portrait photography can be one of the easiest or one of the most challenging types of photography. Almost anyone with a camera can do it, yet it can be a complicated endeavor. Sometimes simply pointing a camera at someone and snapping a picture can create an interesting portrait; other times elaborate lighting setups may be needed to create a mood or to add drama to your subject.

A *portrait,* simply stated, is the likeness of a person — usually the subject's face — whether it is a drawing, a painting, or a photograph. A good portrait should go further than that. It should go beyond simply showing your subject's likeness and delve a bit deeper, hopefully revealing some of your subject's character or emotion also.

You have lots of things to think about when you set out to do a portrait. The first thing to ponder (after you find your subject, of course) is the setting. The setting is the background and surroundings, the place where you shoot the photograph. You need to decide what kind of mood you want to evoke. For example, if you're looking to create a somber mood with a serious model, you may want to try a dark background. For something more festive, you may need a background with a bright color or multiple colors. Your subject may also have some ideas about how they want the image to turn out. Keep an open mind and be ready to try some other ideas that you may have not considered.

There are many ways to evoke a certain mood or ambience in a portrait image. Lighting and background are the principal ways to achieve an effect, but there are other ways. Shooting the image in black and white can give your portrait an evocative feel to it. You can shoot your image so that the colors are more vivid, giving your photo a live, vibrant feeling, or you can tone the colors down for a more ethereal look.

Indoor

Indoor portraits are exactly what they sound like: a portrait shot indoors. One of the biggest obstacles you run into when shooting indoors is that you don't often have enough light to make a good exposure. There are a couple of options you can use to get great indoor shots.

▶ **Use a fast lens.** One of the easiest things you can do is buy a lens with a fast aperture. The 35mm f/1.8 is a great inexpensive fast lens that works well for portraits and all-around photography. The lens I'd recommend the most is the 50mm f/1.4. The 50mm focal length is perfect for shooting portraits and the wide aperture is the fastest you can get with Nikon lenses.

▶ **Window lighting.** Probably the best way you can get great lighting is simply place your subject next to a window. Sunlight filtering through the window is very diffused and makes perfect lighting for portraits. This is a tried-and-true method that many photojournalists and wedding photographers swear by.

7.25 Window lighting is a great way to easily get great lighting.

▶ **Use a Speedlight.** This is usually my last option, but it works well if you use the Speedlight with care. Using bounce flash and a diffuser is essential. If you're planning on using the built-in flash, a diffuser is required or your portrait will come out looking like a snapshot with harsh, flat lighting and bad shadows.

Outdoor

Shooting portraits outdoors has a separate set of difficulties. Unless you're shooting on a completely cloudy day, generally the light is too bright resulting in either blown-out highlights, blocked-up shadows, or in the worst-case scenario, both.

Photographing Children

When taking pictures of children, all the techniques covered earlier still apply. But photographing children, while not completely different than photographing teens or adults, has its own set of difficulties. For one, children tend to move around a lot more than bigger folks, and they are much shorter than we are. These two qualities make the most problems for photographers.

The first issue, moving around, is pretty easily dealt with. Generally you want to shoot with a faster shutter speed to ensure that you get good sharp images even if they're squirming around. The second issue, being short, is something that you must keep in mind. Most people when taking snapshots shoot down at children. This causes them to be looking up and also gives them an odd look due to per-spective distortion. The heads look big and the bodies look too small, which isn't flattering. The key is to remember to get down to the child's level. When you look them in the eye you get much better portraits.

There are a few simple ways to deal with harsh lighting when shooting photos outdoors.

▶ **Find some shade.** Placing your subject out of the direct sun, such as under an overhang or under a tree, can give you the nice soft light that you need. If using a tree, be sure that the coverage is complete as trees can often give you dappled light.

▶ **Use a Speedlight.** I know that this sounds counterintuitive; you're probably thinking, "If I have too much light, why should I add more?" Using the flash in the bright sunlight fills in the dark shadows, resulting in a more evenly exposed image. This technique is known as *fill-flash*.

▶ **Use a diffusion panel.** Another way to combat images that have too much contrast when you're shooting outdoors is to have someone hold a diffusion panel. The diffuser blocks the direct sunlight and acts as a softbox, providing you with a nice soft light for your portrait. Using a reflector to direct some light into the shadow areas of the face works really well, also.

7.26 This shot was taken in the bright sunlight; a diffusion panel was placed between the model and the sun to soften the light.

Portrait photography practice

7.27 Using a Speedlight you can get studio-quality portraits even outdoors.

Table 7.9 Taking Portrait Pictures

Setup	**Practice Picture:** Figure 7.27 is a night portrait I shot in downtown Austin, Texas.
	On Your Own: Part of creating an interesting portrait is having a good background. You can choose to either soften the background or use deep focus to create texture in the image.
Lighting	**Practice Picture:** For this picture I used an off-camera SB-900 controlled by an SU-800. The SB-900 was mounted to a stand and fired through an umbrella. Firing through the umbrella (rather than bouncing) softened the light just a bit so that it retained a relatively hard and directional quality, which was what I was trying to achieve for the retro-noir look of this image.
	On Your Own: Using an off-camera Speedlight can really make your portraits stand out. Using an off-camera TTL cord and an inexpensive SB-400 can get your images looking more like the pros than if you use the flash on-camera.
Lens	**Practice Picture:** Nikon 18-55mm kit lens zoomed to 55mm.
	On Your Own: For portraits you generally want to stay in the longer focal lengths; anywhere from 50 to 105 is recommended.
Camera Settings	**Practice Picture:** I chose Aperture Priority to control the depth of field. I used Spot metering to be sure that some shadow detail was retained. I captured the image in RAW to be able to completely control the conversion to black and white without losing any shadow or highlight detail.
	On Your Own: Controlling your aperture is key in focusing on the details in the image. You may want to use a wide aperture to blur unwanted elements from the background or a small aperture to be sure that the whole scene is in sharp focus.
Exposure	**Practice Picture:** ISO 200 at f/5.6 for 1/60 second. I chose a medium aperture to ensure that some of the details of the wall in the background were in focus.
	On Your Own: When using a Speedlight to shoot portraits, setting your shutter speed anywhere from 1/60 to 1/200 second is recommended. Try to shoot at lower ISO settings to keep as much detail in your image as possible.
Accessories	A small 24-inch umbrella was used to modify the light from the flash.

Portrait photography tips

▶ **Plan some poses.** Take a look at some photos in fashion magazines or even on the Internet and find some poses that you like. Have these in mind when photographing your models.

▶ **Shoot both horizontal and vertical.** Try framing your images in both landscape (horizontal) and portrait (vertical) orientation.

▶ **Try Slow sync flash.** Using Slow sync flash at night can give your images a cool effect.

CHAPTER 8

Viewing, Downloading, and In-camera Editing

With the D3000's large, bright, 3-inch, 230,000-dot VGA LCD monitor, you can view your images and even use the in-camera editing features that allow you to save some time in post-processing and give you the option to fine-tune your images for printing without ever having to download your images to a computer. One interesting option is the ability to make a stop-motion movie that you can view on your computer or share on the Internet via YouTube or Flickr.

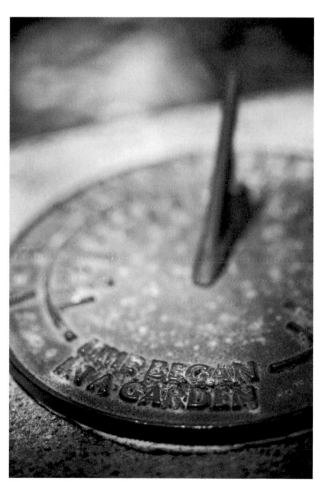

The retouch menu allows you to edit your images without a computer.

Viewing Your Images

The Nikon D3000 offers two ways to view your images while the SD card is still inserted in the camera. You can view the images directly on the LCD monitor on the camera or you can hook up your camera to a standard TV using the Nikon EG-D100 video cable that's available separately from Nikon. You can find the EG-D100 cable at most camera shops or online for around $10.

When viewing through an external device such as a TV, the view is the same as would normally be displayed on the LCD monitor. The camera's buttons and dials function exactly the same.

Before connecting the camera to your television, you need to set the Video out mode. There are two video interface types: PAL and NTSC. These modes control how the electronic signal is processed. In NTSC mode, 30 frames are transmitted each second with each frame being made up of 525 scan lines. PAL mode transmits 25 frames per second with each frame being made up of 625 scan lines. For the most part none of this really matters to you personally; I include the information here as just basic fact. These two different video modes are used in different parts of the world. Most of North and South America use the NTSC mode while Asia and Europe use the PAL video system.

Most of you are going to be located in North America, so you want to set the Video mode to NTSC. If you happen to be located overseas, you probably want to set the Video mode to PAL. If you're unsure whether your TV accepts NTSC or PAL, you should check the owner's manual of your TV.

To set the Video mode:

1. **Turn the camera on.**

2. **Press the Menu button.**

3. **Use the Multi-selector to highlight the Setup menu.**

4. **Use the Multi-selector to highlight Video mode, then press the OK button.**

5. **Use the Multi-selector to highlight NTSC (or PAL).**

6. **Press the OK button to save settings.**

 For more information on playing back images, see Chapter 3.

To connect your camera to a standard TV:

1. **Turn the camera off.** This can prevent damage to your camera's electronics from static electricity.

2. **Open the connector cover.** The connector cover is on the left side of the camera when the lens is facing away from you.

3. **Plug in the EG-D100 video cable.** The cable is available separately from Nikon. Plug the cable into the Video out jack. This is the connection at the top.

4. **Connect the EG-D100 to the input jack of your television or VCR.**

5. **Set your TV to the video channel.** This may differ depending on your TV. See the owner's manual if you are unsure.

6. **Turn on the camera, and press the Playback button.**

Downloading Images

After you finish taking your pictures, you're probably going to want to download them to your computer for further image editing and tweaking or so you can post them to the Web or send them off to your friends and family.

Downloading your images is a fairly simple process, and there are a couple of ways to do this. The most common way is to remove the memory card from the camera and insert it into a card reader that is connected to your computer. This is probably the easiest way to get started. The other option is to use the USB cable supplied with the D3000 and connect the camera directly to the computer. Depending on your computer and the software you have installed, a program might pop up and offer to transfer the image for you. For example, Mac users might find that iPhoto recognizes the camera and opens up once the camera is connected to the computer via the USB cable.

Another option for downloading is using the Nikon Transfer software that was included with the D3000. The Nikon Transfer software is very easy to learn and works well, but I prefer to manually download my images to folders that I have already created to help speed up my workflow. There are times that I forget my card reader so I need to plug the camera in directly, and using the Nikon software just adds another step for me to do. This is a personal preference, and I encourage you to use Nikon Transfer if you don't have a card reader or prefer to plug your camera directly into the computer.

The Retouch Menu

The Nikon D3000 has a very handy Retouch menu. These in-camera editing options make it simple for you to print straight from the camera without downloading it to your computer or using any image-editing software.

One great feature of using the Retouch menu is that the camera saves the retouched image as a copy so you don't lose the original image. This can be beneficial if you decide that you would rather edit the photo on your computer or if you simply aren't happy with the outcome. There are two ways to access the Retouch menu.

The first and quickest method:

1. **Press the Play button to enter Playback mode.** Your most recently taken image appears on the LCD screen.

2. **Use the Multi-selector to review your images.**

3. **When you see an image you want to retouch, press the OK button to display the Retouch menu options.**

4. **Use the Multi-selector to highlight the Retouch option you want to use.** Depending on the Retouch option you choose, you may have to select additional settings.

5. **Make adjustments if necessary.**

6. **Press the OK button to save.**

The second method:

1. **Press the Menu button to view menu options.**

2. **Use the Multi-selector to scroll down to the Retouch menu.** It's the fourth menu down and appears as an icon with a paintbrush.

8.1 The Retouch menu

3. **Press the Multi-selector right, then use the Multi-selector up and down buttons to highlight the Retouch option you want to use.** Depending on the Retouch option you select, you may have to select additional settings. Once you have selected your option(s), thumbnails appear.

4. **Use the Multi-selector to select the image to retouch, and then press the OK button.**

5. **Make the necessary adjustments.**

6. **Press the OK button to save.**

Retouch Menu Options

There are a few options you can select when using the Retouch menu. The options vary from cropping your image to adjusting the color balance to taking red-eye out of your pictures and even to processing RAW images.

D-Lighting

This allows you to adjust the image by brightening the shadows. This is not the same as Active D-lighting. D-Lighting uses a curves adjustment to help to bring out details in the shadow areas of an image. This option is for use with backlit subjects or images that may be slightly underexposed.

8.2 The D-Lighting option

When the D-Lighting option is chosen from the Retouch menu, you can use the Multi-selector to choose a thumbnail and the Zoom in button to get a closer look at the image. Press the OK button to choose the image to retouch, and two thumbnails are displayed; one is the original image, and the other is the image with D-Lighting applied.

You can use the Multi-selector up or down to select the amount of D-Lighting: Low, Normal, or High. The results can be viewed in real time and compared with the original before saving. Press the OK button to save, the Playback button to cancel, and the Zoom in button to view the full-frame image.

Red-eye correction

This option enables the camera to automatically correct for the red-eye effect that can sometimes be caused by using the flash on pictures taken of people. This option is only available on photos taken with flash. When choosing images to retouch from the Playback menu by pressing the OK button during preview, this option is grayed out and cannot be selected if the camera detects that a flash was not used. When attempting to choose an image directly from the Retouch menu, a message is displayed stating that this image cannot be used.

Once the image has been selected, press the OK button; the camera then automatically corrects the red-eye and saves a copy of the image to your SD card.

If an image is selected that flash was used on but there is no red-eye present, the camera displays a message stating that red-eye is not detected in the image and no retouching will be done.

Trim

This option allows you to crop your image to remove distracting elements or to allow you to crop closer to the subject. You can also use the Zoom in and Zoom out buttons to adjust the size of the crop. This allows you to crop closer in or farther out depending on your needs.

Use the Multi-selector to move the crop around the image so you can center the crop on the part of the image that you think is most important. When you are happy with the crop you have selected, press the OK button to save a copy of your cropped image or press the Playback button to return to the main menu without saving.

Rotating the Command dial allows you to choose different aspect ratios for your crop. You can choose the aspect ratio to conform to different print sizes. The options are

- ▶ **3:2.** This is the default crop size. This ratio is good for prints sized 4 × 6, 8 × 12, and 12 × 18.
- ▶ **4:3.** This is the ratio for prints sized 6 × 8 or 12 × 18.
- ▶ **5:4.** This is the standard size for 8 × 10 prints.
- ▶ **1:1.** This gives you a square crop.
- ▶ **16:9.** This is what's known as a cinematic crop. This is the ratio that movie screens and widescreen televisions use.

Monochrome

This option allows you to make a copy of your color image in a monochrome format. There are three options:

▶ **Black-and-white.** This changes your image to shades of black, white, and gray.

▶ **Sepia.** This gives your image the look of a black-and-white photo that has been sepia toned. Sepia toning is a traditional photographic process that gives the photo a reddish-brown tint.

▶ **Cyanotype.** This option gives your photos a blue or cyan tint. Cyanotypes are a form of processing film-based photographic images.

When using the Sepia or Cyanotype, you can use the Multi-selector up and down buttons to adjust the lightness or darkness of the effect. Press the OK button to save a copy of the image or press the Playback button to cancel without saving.

The Monochrome Picture Control offers more flexible settings than simply retouching the images using the Retouch menu. You may want to consider shooting your images using the Picture Control rather than using this option.

8.3 An image converted to black and white.

8.4 An image converted to sepia.

8.5 An image converted to cyanotype.

Filter effects

Filter effects allow you to simulate the effects of using certain filters over your lens to subtly modify the colors of your image. There are seven filter effects available:

▶ **Skylight.** A skylight filter is used to absorb some of the UV rays emitted by the sun. The UV rays can give your image a slightly bluish tint. Using the skylight filter effect causes your image to be less blue.

▶ **Warm filter.** A warming filter adds a little orange to your image to give it a warmer hue. This filter effect can sometimes be useful when using flash because flash can sometimes cause your images to feel a little too cool.

▶ **Red intensifier.** This adds a red colorcast to your image. You can use the Multi-selector up or down to lighten or darken the effect.

▶ **Green intensifier.** This adds a green colorcast to your image. You can use the Multi-selector up or down to lighten or darken the effect.

▶ **Blue intensifier.** This adds a blue colorcast to your image. You can use the Multi-selector up or down to lighten or darken the effect.

▶ **Cross screen.** This effect simulates the use of a star filter. A star filter creates a star-shaped pattern on the bright highlights in your image. If your image doesn't have any bright highlights, the effect will not be apparent. Once an image is selected for the cross screen filter, you are shown a submenu with a few options that you can adjust. You can choose the number of points on the stars: 4, 6, or 8. You can also choose the amount; there are three settings that give you more or fewer stars. You can choose three angle settings, which control the angle at which the star is tilted. You also have three settings that control the length of the points on the stars.

▶ **Soft.** This applies a soft glow to your images. This effect is mostly used for portraiture but can also be used effectively for landscapes as well.

After choosing the desired filter effect, press the OK button to save a copy of your image with the effect added.

8.6 Cross screen filter

Color balance

You can use the color balance option to create a copy of an image on which you have adjusted the color balance. Using this option, you can use the Multi-selector to add a color tint to your image. You can use this effect to neutralize an existing color tint or to add a color tint for artistic purposes.

Press the Multi-selector up to increase the amount of green, down to increase the amount of magenta, left to add blue, and right to add amber.

8.7 Color chart and histograms using the color balance option

A color chart and color histograms are displayed along with an image preview so you can see how the color balance affects your image. When you are satisfied with your image, press the OK button to save a copy.

Small picture

This is a handy little option that allows you to make a copy of your images that are a smaller size. These smaller pictures are more suitable for e-mailing to friends and family.

The first thing you need to do when creating a small picture is to select the Choose size option from the Small picture submenu. You have three sizes to choose from: 640 × 480, 320 × 240, or 160 × 120. After you decide on what size you want your small pictures copied, go to the Select picture option. When the Select picture option is chosen, the LCD displays thumbnails of all of the images in the current folder. To scroll through your images, use the Multi-selector left or right. To select or deselect an image, use the Multi-selector up or down. You can select as many images as you have on your memory card. When all the images that you want to make a small copy of are selected, press the OK button to make the copies.

Image overlay

This option allows you to combine two RAW images and save them as one. This menu option can only be accessed by entering the Retouch menu using the Menu button (the longer route); you cannot access this option by pressing the OK button when in Playback mode.

To use this option, you must have at least two RAW images saved to your memory card. This option is not available for use with JPEG.

To use this option:

1. **Press the Menu button to view the menu options.**

2. **Use the Multi-selector to scroll down to the Retouch menu, and press the Multi-selector right to enter the Retouch menu.**

3. **Use the Multi-selector up or down to highlight Image Overlay.**

4. **Press the Multi-selector right.** This displays the Image Overlay menu.

5. **Press the OK button to view RAW image thumbnails.** Use the Multi-selector to highlight the first RAW image to be used in the overlay. Press the OK button to select it.

6. **Adjust the exposure of Image 1 by pressing the Multi-selector up or down.** Press the OK button when the image is adjusted to your liking.

7. **Press the Multi-selector right to switch to Image 2.**

8. **Press the OK button to view RAW image thumbnails.** Use the Multi-selector to highlight the second RAW image to be used in the overlay. Press the OK button to select it.

9. **Adjust the exposure of Image 2 by pressing the Multi-selector up or down.** Press the OK button when the image is adjusted to your liking.

10. **Press the Multi-selector right to highlight the Preview window.**

11. **Press the Multi-selector up or down to highlight Overlay to preview the image, or use the Multi-selector to highlight Save to save the image without previewing.**

NEF (RAW) processing

This option allows you to do some basic editing to images saved in the RAW format without downloading them to a computer and using image-editing software. This option is limited in its function but allows you to fine-tune your image more precisely when printing straight from the camera or memory card.

You can save a copy of your image in JPEG format. You can choose the image quality and size that the copy is saved as, you can adjust the white balance settings, fine-tune the exposure compensation, and select a Picture Control setting to be applied.

To apply RAW processing:

1. **Enter the NEF (RAW) Processing menu through the Retouch menu.** Press the OK button to view thumbnails of the images stored on your card. Only images saved in RAW format will be displayed.

2. **Use the Multi-selector left or right to scroll through the thumbnails.** Press the OK button to select the highlighted image. This brings up a dialog screen with the image adjustment submenu located to the right of the image you have selected.

8.8 NEF (RAW) processing menu screen

3. **Use the Multi-selector up or down to highlight the adjustment you want to make.** You can set Image quality, Image size, White balance, Exposure compensation, and Optimize image. You can also use the Zoom in button to view a full screen preview.

4. **When you have made your adjustments, use the Multi-selector to highlight EXE and press the OK button to save changes or the Playback button to cancel without saving.** EXE sets the changes and saves a copy of the image in JPEG format at the size and quality that you have selected. The camera default saves the image as a Large, Fine JPEG.

For more information on image size, quality, white balance, and exposure compensation, see Chapter 2.

Quick retouch

The Quick retouch option is the easiest option. The camera automatically adjusts the contrast and saturation making your image brighter and more colorful, perfect for printing straight from the camera or memory card. In the event that your image is dark or backlit, the camera also automatically applies D-Lighting to help bring out details in the shadow areas of your picture.

Once your image has been selected for Quick retouch, you have the option to choose how much of the effect is applied. You can choose from High, Normal, or Low. The LCD monitor displays a side-by side comparison between the image as shot and the image retouched to give you a better idea of what the effect looks like.

Once you decide how much of the effect you want, press the OK button to save a copy of the retouched image or you can press the Playback button to cancel without making any changes to your picture.

Color outline

The color outline feature takes the selected image and creates an outline copy that can be opened using image-editing software, such as Photoshop or Corel Paintshop Pro, and colored in by hand. This option works best when used on an image with high contrast.

Miniature effect

This effect is modeled after a technique that some people call (erroneously) the "tilt-shift effect" because it can be achieved optically with a tilt-shift lens. Quite simply what this effect does is simulate the shallow depth of field normally present in macro shots. This tricks the eye into seeing something large as something very tiny. The effect only works with very far-off subjects and works better when the vantage point is looking down. It's a pretty cool effect but only works with limited subjects, so use this effect with that in mind.

Stop-motion movie

This option allows you to link together up to 100 images to be shown in a series and saved as a movie (AVI) file. Stop motion is used in animation to make still objects appear as if they are moving, similar to cartoon animation. Basically how it works is you take a shot of an object, move it slightly, take another shot, and so on. After these images are linked and played, the still object appears to move. The effect is sort of a crude, jerky animation. I don't find the need to use this option very often, but if you have some time and patience, I'm sure you could put together some very interesting short movies.

Some other ways to use this feature would be to shoot an action sequence such as a skateboarder jumping a ramp and link it together to show the motion or even to put together a quick slide show of random images from your memory card. Follow these steps:

1. **After shooting a sequence of images, go to the Stop-motion movies option in the Retouch menu and press the OK button.** This brings you to a menu screen that gives you the options of Create movie, Frame size, and Frame rate.

2. **Select Frame size.** This allows you to choose how large the still frames in your movie are. The choices are

   - **640 × 480.** This option stores your images at 640 pixels × 480 pixels. This is a suitable size for viewing on a small TV or computer monitor. This option results in a rather large file size.

   - **320 × 240.** This option is more suitable for posting to your Web site or to a site that hosts video, such as YouTube or Flickr.

   - **160 × 120.** This gives you the smallest file size and is suitable for e-mailing.

3. **After you set your frame size, use the Multi-selector to scroll down to Frame rate and press the OK button.** This gives you the options for the frame rate. The frame rate, given in frames per second (fps), is how many still images are shown per second. There are four options:

   - **15 fps.** This is the highest option and, generally speaking, 15 fps is about the minimum acceptable frame rate you can use before your movie appears jerky.

   - **10 fps.** This shows you ten images per second and appears somewhat jerky.

   - **6 fps.** This shows you six images per second. The video appears very jerky.

   - **3 fps.** This shows three images per second.

4. **After you choose your frame size and rate, use the Multi-selector to scroll up to Create movie and press the OK button.** This brings you to a menu screen where you choose a starting image and a stopping image for your movie.

5. **Using the Multi-selector, choose the image you want to start on and press the OK button to select it.**

6. **Using the Multi-selector, choose the image you want to stop on and press the OK button.**

7. **If you are happy with your choices, press the OK button again to save or use the Multi-selector button to highlight Edit, and then Press OK to make new choices.**

8. **After you save your ending point, you are shown yet another menu.** There are four options:

   - **Save.** This option allows you to instantly save the stop-motion movie file to your memory card.

- **Preview.** This allows you to view the stop-motion movie on your LCD monitor before saving to the memory card.

- **Frame rate.** This allows you to adjust the frame rate as before: 15 fps, 10 fps, 6 fps, or 3 fps.

- **Edit.** This allows you to change the starting and ending frame as well as to choose to not show certain frames in the middle. To choose not to show middle frames, select the Middle frame option, then use the Multi-selector left and right to scroll through the thumbnails. Use the Multi-selector up and down to set the images to be shown or not. A small check mark appears in the images to be shown; deselecting the image deletes it from playback (but not from the memory card).

Side by side comparison

This option allows you to view a side-by-side comparison of the retouched image and the original copy of the image. This option can only be accessed by selecting an image that has been retouched.

To use this option:

1. **Press the Play button and use the Multi-selector to choose the retouched image to view.**

2. **Press the OK button to display the Retouch menu.**

3. **Use the Multi-selector to highlight Before and after, and then press the OK button.**

4. **Use the Multi-selector to highlight either the original or retouched image. You can then use the Zoom in button to view closer.**

5. **Press the Play button to exit the Before and after comparison and return to Playback mode.**

Accessories

There are a number of accessories and additional equipment that are available for the Nikon D3000. These accessories range from batteries and flashes to tripods and camera bags. They can enhance your shooting experience by providing you with options that aren't immediately available with the purchase of the camera alone.

ML-L3 Wireless Remote Control

This relatively inexpensive and handy little device is used to wirelessly trigger the shutter release on the D3000 using the infrared sensor located on the front of the camera. To use this feature, set the camera Drive mode to Remote (you can choose from Quick Response remote or Delayed remote). Point the remote at the camera and press the button.

This remote is great for triggering the camera when you want to do self-portraits or if you want to get in the picture when doing a group portrait. This remote is also very useful to use to reduce camera shake when doing long exposures with the camera mounted on a tripod.

> **NOTE** The Bulb setting is unavailable when the camera is set to one of the remote drive modes. You do, however, get a setting called *Time*. When set to this, press the remote button once to open the shutter and once again to close the shutter.

Tripods

One of the most important accessories you can have for your camera, whether you're a professional or just a hobbyist, is a tripod. The tripod allows you to get sharper

Image courtesy of Nikon, Inc.
A.1 ML-L3 wireless remote

images by eliminating the shake caused by handholding the camera in low-light situations. A tripod can also allow you to use a lower ISO, thereby reducing the camera noise and resulting in an image with better resolution.

There are literally hundreds of types of tripods available, ranging in size from less than 6 inches to one that extends all the way up to 6 feet or more. In general, the heavier the tripod is, the better it is at keeping the camera steady. The Nikon D3000 is a relatively small camera, so you may not need a heavy-duty tripod. A smaller light-weight tripod will suffice for most shooting conditions.

While you can spend $500 or more on a state-of-the-art carbon-fiber tripod with a magnesium pistol-grip ball head, you may not need all these bells and whistles. Just remember, however, that you get what you pay for, and in the long run if you buy a better tripod, you will be much happier than if you just buy a $20 flimsy tripod. For quite a few years when I was starting out, I used a hand-me-down tripod that was probably quite good in its day and I also used cheap lightweight aluminum tripods. I was always disappointed and annoyed to say the least. When I finally broke down and bought a new, fairly expensive tripod and head, I was surprised to find that I didn't mind bringing the tripod with me because it was much quicker and easier to use while being sturdier as well. Bottom line is, don't skimp when buying a tripod; a good sturdy tripod will last you for many years.

There are many different features available on tripods, but the standard features include:

▶ **Height.** This is an important feature. The tripod should be the right height for the specific application for which you are using it. If you are shooting landscapes most of the time and you are 6 feet tall, using a 4-foot-tall tripod will force you to bend over to look into the viewfinder to compose your image. This may not be the optimal size tripod for you.

▶ **Head.** Tripods have several types of heads. The most common type of head is the *pan/tilt* head. This type of head allows you to rotate, or *pan*, with a moving subject and also allows you to tilt the camera for angled or vertical shots. The other common type of head on a tripod is the *ball* head. The ball head is the most versatile. It can tilt and rotate quickly into nearly any position. In addition there are also different types of ball heads: a standard ball that has a simple locking mechanism that screws down, or a pistol grip that has a grip and a lever that you squeeze to quickly move the head and simply release to lock it into place. I prefer a pistol-grip ball head.

▶ **Plate.** The plate attaches the camera to the tripod. The Nikon D3000 has a threaded socket on the bottom. Tripods have a type of bolt that screws into these sockets, and this bolt is on the plate. Most decent tripods have what is called a *quick release* plate. You can remove a quick-release plate from the tripod and attach it to the camera and then reattach it to the tripod with a locking mechanism. If you're going to be taking the camera on and off of the tripod frequently, this is the most time-efficient type of plate to use. The other type of plate, which is on some inexpensive tripods, is the standard type of plate that is attached directly to the head of the tripod. It still has the screw bolt that attaches the camera to the plate,

A.2 A tripod ball head with a pistol grip

but it is much more time-consuming to use when you plan to take the camera on and off a lot. You must screw the camera to the plate every time you want to use the tripod, and you must unscrew it when you want to remove it from the tripod.

When to use a tripod

There are many situations when using a tripod is ideal, and the most obvious is when it's dark or lighting is poor. However, using a tripod even when there is ample light can help keep your image sharp. The following are just a few ideas of when you may want to use a tripod:

▶ **When the light is low.** Your camera needs a longer shutter speed to get the proper exposure if there isn't much available light. The problem is, when the shutter speed gets longer, you need steadier hands to get sharp exposures. Attaching your camera to a tripod eliminates camera shake.

▶ **When the camera is zoomed in.** When you use a long focal-length lens, the shaking of your hands is more exaggerated due to the higher magnification of the scene and can cause your images to be blurry, even in moderate light.

▶ **When shooting landscapes.** Landscape shots, especially when you use the Landscape scene mode, require a smaller aperture to get maximum depth of field to ensure that the whole scene is in focus. When the camera is using a smaller aperture, the shutter speed can be long enough to suffer from camera shake, even when the day is bright.

▶ **When shooting close up.** When the camera is very close to a subject, camera shake can also be magnified. When you shoot close-ups or macro shots, it may also be preferable to use a smaller aperture to increase depth of field, thus lengthening the shutter speed.

Which tripod is right for you?

Considering there are so many types of tripods, choosing one can be a daunting experience. There are many features and functions available in a tripod; here are some things to think about when you're looking into purchasing one:

▶ **Price.** Tripods can range in price from as little as $5 to as much as $500 or more. Obviously, the more a tripod costs, the more features and stability it's likely to have. Look closely at your needs when deciding what price level to focus on.

▶ **Features.** There are dozens of different features available in any given tripod. Some tripods have a quick-release plate, some have a ball head, some are small, and some are large. Again, you need to decide what your specific needs are.

▶ **Weight.** This can be a very important factor when deciding which tripod to purchase. If you are going to use the tripod mostly in your home, a heavy tripod may not be a problem. On the other hand, if you plan on hiking, a 7-pound tripod can be an encumbrance after awhile. Some manufacturers make tripods that are made out of carbon fiber. While these tripods are very stable, they are also extremely lightweight. On the downside, carbon-fiber tripods are also very expensive.

▶ **Locking mechanism.** There are a couple types of locking mechanisms found on today's tripods. The two most common are the twist-lock and the lever-lock. The twist-lock functions by twisting a collar that allows the leg to telescope. The lever-lock functions by simply flipping a lever up to release the telescoping leg and down again to lock the leg. Personally, I prefer the lever-lock types for the ease and quickness with which they operate.

Monopods

An option you may want to consider is a *monopod* instead of a tripod. A monopod connects to the camera the same way as a tripod, but it only has one leg. Monopods are excellent for shooting sports and action with long lenses, because they allow you the freedom to move along with support to keep your camera steady. The figure here shows a photographer using a monopod to photograph racecars.

Photo © Destry Jaimes – nine2fivephotography.com

Tripods have legs made from different types of materials. Each tripod has its own features that make it useful for specific purposes. Some types of materials include:

▶ **Wood.** Wooden tripods aren't seen very much anymore. These were the tripods of choice for photographers from the past who used large, heavy, box-like view cameras or field cameras. These wood tripods are often heavy, but they support quite a bit of weight and are also good at dampening vibrations, which can cause camera shake.

▶ **Aluminum.** Most of the tripods on the market today are made from aluminum. Aluminum is a lightweight and durable material that's fairly low in cost. This is the most cost-effective type of tripod, although depending on the feature set of the tripod, some can get pretty expensive.

▶ **Carbon fiber.** These tripods are made from layers of cross-plied carbon fiber, which is a great material. Carbon fiber is significantly (20 to 30 percent) lighter than aluminum and dampens vibrations much better than wooden tripods do. Tripods with carbon-fiber legs are some of the most expensive ones, but they are very durable and are perfect for when you're hiking because of their light weight.

▶ **Exotic materials.** Some tripod manufacturers, such as Giotto's and Gitzo, use materials such as basalt, which comes from molten lava, to make their tripod legs. The basalt is crushed, melted, and then drawn into fibers similar to carbon fiber.

Camera Bags and Cases

Another important accessory to consider is the bag or carrying case you choose for your camera. These can provide protection not only from the elements but also from impact. Camera bags and cases exist for any kind of use you can imagine, from simple cases to prevent scratches to elaborate camera bags that can hold everything you may need for a week's vacation. Being a freelance photographer, I get jobs that require different amounts of gear so I have quite a few camera bags. Some of the bag and case types available include:

▶ **Hard cases.** These are some of the best cases you can get. These cases are generally made to take heavy abuse and are commonly used for shipping camera equipment. The most recognizable name in hard cases is the Pelican brand. The Pelican hard cases are watertight, crushproof, and dustproof. They are unconditionally guaranteed forever. If you are hard on your cameras or do a lot of outdoors activities, you can't go wrong with these. Recently, Pelican started to offer soft camera bags; obviously they aren't waterproof and crushproof, but they are excellent bags, nonetheless.

▶ **Shoulder bags.** These are the standard camera bags you can find at any camera shop. They come in a multitude of sizes to fit almost any amount of equipment you can carry. Reputable makers include Tamrac, Domke, and Lowepro. Look them up on the Web to peruse the various styles and sizes. I use a couple of different shoulder bags depending on the job. For traveling with my camera gear and a laptop I use the Naneu Pro Tango, but if I'm only carrying camera gear, the Correspondent C330 usually fits everything I need.

▶ **Backpacks.** Some camera cases are made to be worn on your back just like a standard backpack. These also come in different sizes and styles, and some even offer laptop-carrying capabilities. The type of camera backpack I use when traveling is a Naneu Pro Alpha. It's designed to look like a military pack, so thieves don't know you're carrying camera equipment. When traveling, I usually pack it up with two Nikon dSLR camera bodies, a wide-angle zoom, a long tele-photo, a couple of prime lenses, two Speedlights, a reflector disk, and all the chargers, batteries, and other accessories that go along with my gear. And, with all that equipment packed away, there is space left over for a lunch. Lowepro and Tamrac also make some very excellent backpacks.

▶ **Messenger bags.** Recently more camera bag manufacturers have started to offer messenger bags, which resemble the types of bags that a bike messenger uses. They have one strap that goes over your shoulder and across your chest. The bag sits on your back like a backpack. The good thing about these bags is that you can just grab it and pull it around to the front for easy access to your gear. With a back-pack, you have to take it off to get to your camera. I also have one of these for when I'm travel-ing light. My messenger bag is the Echo made by Naneu Pro.

▶ **Holster type bags.** The holster-type camera bag is a bare-bones camera holder. It's made to carry one camera with a lens attached and a few accessories, such as batteries and flash cards. In my opinion, the best holster-type bag is the Lowepro Toploader. Lowepro makes several types of holsters to accommodate differ-ent cameras and lens combina-tions. These bags are great for protecting your gear when you're traveling with a small amount of equipment on a day trip.

Image courtesy of NaneuPro
AA.3 Naneu Pro Alpha backpack

Image courtesy of NaneuPro
AA.4 Naneu Pro Echo messenger bag

Resources

There is a lot of valuable information available on the Internet for photographers. This appendix is a resource to help you discover some of the many ways to learn more about the Nikon D3000 and about photography in general.

Informational Web Sites

With the amount of information on the Web, sometimes it is difficult to know where to look or where to begin. These are a few sites that I suggest you start with when looking for reliable information about your D3000 or photography in general.

Nikonusa.com

The Nikon Web site is a great resource when you want to access the technical specifications for Nikon Speedlights, cameras, or lenses. You can also find firmware updates or possible recalls. Visit http://nikonusa.com.

Nikonians.org

This site is a forum where you can post questions and discussion topics for other Nikon users about a range of photography-related topics. Visit www.nikonians.org.

Photo.net

Photo.net is a large site containing resources from equipment reviews, to forums on a variety of topics, to tutorials, and more. If you are looking for specific photography-related information and aren't sure where to look, this is a great place to start. Visit http://photo.net.

J. Dennis Thomas' Digital Field Guide Companion

This is a blog that I publish. I post different tips and tricks as well as updates from Nikon and lots of other tidbits of information. Visit http://deadsailorproductions.com.

Workshops

There are a multitude of workshops that offer training for photographers. Here is a list of some of the workshops that are available to you.

Ansel Adams Gallery Workshops

http://anseladams.com

Brooks Institute Weekend Workshops

http://workshops.brooks.edu

Great American Photography Workshops

http://www.gaphotoworks.com/

Mentor Series Worldwide Photo Treks

http://mentorseries.com

Photo Quest Adventures

http://www.photoquestadventures.com/

Summit Series of Photography Workshops

http://photographyatthesummit.com

Santa Fe Photographic Workshops

http://santafeworkshops.com

Nikon School & Workshops

www.nikonschool.com

Online Photography Magazines and Other Photo-Related Sites

Some photography magazines also have Web sites that offer photography articles and often information that isn't found in the pages of the magazine. The following is a list of Web sites of a few photography magazines as well as some other photo-related sites where you may find useful content.

Digital Photographer
http://digiphotomag.com

Digital Photo Pro
http://digitalphotopro.com

Flickr
http://flickr.com

Outdoor Photographer
http://outdoorphotographer.com

Photo District News
http://pdnonline.com

Popular Photography & Imaging
http://popularphotography.com

Shutterbug
http://shutterbug.net

How to Use the Gray Card and Color Checker

Have you ever wondered how some photographers are able to consistently produce photos with such accurate color and exposure? It's often because they use gray cards and color checkers. Knowing how to use these tools helps you take some of the guesswork out of capturing photos with great color and correct exposures every time.

The Gray Card

Because the color of light changes depending on the light source, what you might decide is neutral in your photograph, isn't neutral at all. This is where a gray card comes in very handy. A gray card is designed to reflect the color spectrum neutrally in all sorts of lighting conditions, providing a standard from which to measure for later color corrections or to set a custom white balance.

By taking a test shot that includes the gray card, you guarantee that you have a neutral item to adjust colors against later if you need to. Make sure that the card is placed in the same light that the subject is for the first photo, and then remove the gray card and continue shooting.

 When taking a photo of a gray card, de-focus your lens a little; this ensures that you capture a more even color.

Because many software programs enable you to address color correction issues by choosing something that should be white or neutral in an image, having the gray card in the first of a series of photos allows you to select the gray card as the neutral point. Your software resets red, green and blue to be the same value, creating a neutral mid-tone. Depending on the capabilities of your software, you might be able to save the adjustment you've made and apply it to all other photos shot in the same series.

If you'd prefer to made adjustments on the spot, for example, and if the lighting conditions will remain mostly consistent while you shoot a large number of images, it is advisable to use the gray card to set a custom white balance in your camera. You can do this by taking a photo of the gray card filling as much of the frame as possible. Then, use that photo to set the custom white balance.

The Color Checker

A color checker contains 24 swatches which represent colors found in everyday scenes, including skin tones, sky, foliage, etc. It also contains red, green, blue, cyan, magenta and yellow, which are used in all printing devices. Finally, and perhaps most importantly, it has six shades of gray.

Using a color checker is a very similar process to using a gray card. You place it in the scene so that it is illuminated in the same way as the subject. Photograph the scene once with the reference in place, then remove it and continue shooting. You should create a reference photo each time you shoot in a new lighting environment.

Later on in software, open the image containing the color checker. Measure the values of the gray, black, and white swatches. The red, green and blue values in the gray swatch should each measure around 128, in the black swatch around 50, and in the white swatch around 245. If your camera's white balance was set correctly for the scene, your measurements should fall into the range (and deviate by no more than 7 either way) and you can rest easy knowing your colors are true.

If your readings are more than 7 points out of range either way, use software to correct it. But now you also have black and white reference points to help. Use the levels adjustment tool to bring the known values back to where they should be measuring (gray around 128, black around 50 and white around 245).

If your camera offers any kind of custom styles, you can also use the color checker to set or adjust any of the custom styles by taking a sample photo and evaluating it using the on-screen histogram, preferably the RGB histogram if your camera offers one. You can then choose that custom style for your shoot, perhaps even adjusting that custom style to better match your expectations for color.

Glossary

Active D-Lighting A camera setting that preserves highlight and shadow details in a high-contrast scene with a wide dynamic range.

AE (Autoexposure) A function of a camera where the camera selects the aperture and/or shutter speed according to the camera's built-in light meter. See also *Aperture Priority*, *Shutter Priority*, and *Programmed Auto*.

AE/AF (Autoexposure/Autofocus) Lock A camera control that lets you lock the current metered exposure and/or autofocus setting prior to taking a photo. This allows you to meter an off-center subject and then recompose the shot while retaining the proper exposure for the subject. The function of this button can be altered in the setup menu.

AF-assist illuminator An LED light that's emitted in low-light or low-contrast situations. The AF-assist illuminator provides enough light for the camera's AF to work in low light.

ambient lighting Lighting that naturally exists in a scene.

angle of view The area of a scene that a lens can capture, which is determined by the focal length of the lens. Lenses with a shorter focal length have a wider angle of view than lenses with a longer focal length.

aperture The opening of the lens similar to the iris of an eye. The designation for each step in the aperture is called the f-stop. The smaller the f-stop (or f-number), the larger the actual opening of the aperture; and the higher-numbered f-stops designate smaller apertures, letting in less light. The f-number is the ratio of the focal length to the aperture diameter.

Aperture Priority An exposure mode setting where you choose the aperture and the camera automatically adjusts the shutter speed according to the camera's metered readings. Aperture Priority is often used by a photographer to control depth of field.

aspect ratio The ratio of the long edge of an image to the short edge as printed, displayed on a monitor, or captured by a digital camera.

autofocus The capability of a camera to determine the proper focus of the subject automatically.

backlighting A lighting effect produced when the main light source is located behind the subject. Backlighting can be used to create a silhouette effect or to illuminate translucent objects. See also *frontlighting* and *sidelighting*.

barrel distortion An aberration in a lens in which the lines at the edges and sides of the image are bowed outward. This distortion is usually found in shorter focal-length (wide-angle) lenses.

bounce flash Pointing the flash head in an upward position or toward a wall so that it bounces off another surface before reaching the subject, which softens the light reaching the subject. This often eliminates shadows and provides smoother light for portraits.

bracketing A photographic technique in which you vary the exposure over two or more frames. By doing this, you ensure a proper exposure in difficult lighting situations where your camera's meter can be fooled.

broad lighting When your main light is illuminating the side of the subject that's facing toward you.

camera shake Camera movement, usually at slower shutter speeds, which produces a blurred image.

catchlight Highlights that appear in the subject's eyes.

center-weighted meter A light-measuring device that emphasizes the area in the middle of the frame when you're calculating the correct exposure for an image.

colored gel filters Colored translucent filters that are placed over a flash head or light to change the color of the light emitted on the subject. Colored gels can be used to create a colored hue of an image. Gels are often used to match the flash output with the ambient light as well as to change the color of a background when shooting portraits or still lifes by placing the gel over the flash head and then firing the flash at the background.

compression Reducing the size of a file by digital encoding, which uses fewer bits of information to represent the original subject. Some compression types, such as JPEG, actually discard some image information, while others, such as RAW (NEF), preserve all the details in the original.

Continuous Autofocus (AF-C) A camera setting that allows the camera to continually focus on a moving subject.

contrast The range between the lightest and darkest tones in an image. In a high-contrast image, the shades fall at the extremes of the range between white and black. In a low-contrast image, the tones are closer together.

dedicated flash An electronic flash unit, such as the Nikon SB-900, SB-800, SB-600, or SB-400, designed to work with the autoexposure features of a specific camera.

depth of field (DOF) The portion of a scene from foreground to background that appears sharp in the image.

diffuse lighting A soft, low-contrast lighting.

D-Lighting A function within the camera that can fix the underexposure that often happens to images that are backlit or in deep shadow. This is accomplished by adjusting the levels of the image after it's been captured. Not to be confused with Active D-Lighting.

DX Nikon's designation for digital single-lens reflex cameras (dSLRs) that use an APS-C–sized (23.6mm × 15.8mm) sensor.

equivalent focal length A DX-format digital camera's focal length, which is translated into the corresponding values for 35mm film or the FX format.

exposure The amount of light allowed to reach the sensor, which is determined by the ISO setting, the amount admitted by the aperture of the lens, and the length of time determined by the shutter speed.

exposure compensation A technique for adjusting the exposure indicated by a photographic exposure meter, in consideration of factors that may cause the indicated exposure to result in a less-than-optimal image.

exposure mode Camera settings that control how the exposure settings are determined. The D3000 also offers Scene modes, which are automatic modes that adjust the settings to predetermined parameters, such as a wide aperture for the Portrait. See also *Aperture priority*, *Shutter priority*, and *Programmed Auto*.

fill flash A lighting technique where the Speedlight provides enough light to illuminate the subject to eliminate shadows. Using a flash for outdoor portraits often brightens the subject in conditions where the camera meters light from a broader scene.

fill lighting The lighting used to illuminate shadows. Reflectors or additional incandescent lighting or electronic flash can be used to brighten shadows. One common outdoor technique is to use the camera's flash as a fill.

flash An external light source that produces an almost instant flash of light to illuminate a scene. Also known as electronic flash.

Flash Exposure Compensation (FEC) Adjusting the flash output. If images are too dark (underexposed), you can use FEC to increase the flash output. If images are too bright (overexposed), you can use FEC to reduce the flash output.

flash modes Modes that enable you to control the output of the flash by using different parameters. Some of these modes include Red-Eye Reduction and Slow Sync.

flash output level The output level of the flash as determined by one of the Flash modes used.

Front-curtain sync Front-curtain sync causes the flash to fire at the beginning of this period when the shutter is completely open in the instant that the first curtain of the focal plane shutter finishes its movement across the film or sensor plane. This is the default setting. See also *Rear-curtain sync*.

frontlighting The illumination coming from the direction of the camera. See also *backlighting* and *sidelighting*.

f-stop See *aperture*.

histogram A graphic representation of the range of tones in an image.

hot shoe The slot located on the top of the camera where the flash connects. The hot shoe is considered hot because it has electronic contacts that allow communication between the flash and the camera.

ISO sensitivity The ISO (International Organization for Standardization) setting on the camera indicates the light sensitivity. In digital cameras, lower ISO settings provide better quality images with less image noise; however, a lower ISO setting requires more exposure time.

JPEG (Joint Photographic Experts Group) This is an image format that compresses the image data from the camera to achieve a smaller file size. The compression algorithm discards some of the detail when closing the image. The degree of compression can be adjusted, allowing a selectable tradeoff between storage size and image quality. JPEG is the most common image format used by digital cameras and other photographic image-capture devices.

Kelvin A unit of measurement of color temperature based on a theoretical black body that glows a specific color when heated to a certain temperature. The sun is approximately 5500 K.

lag time The length of time between when the Shutter Release button is pressed and the shutter is actually released; the lag time on the D3000 is so short, it's almost imperceptible. Compact digital cameras are notorious for having long lag times, which can cause you to miss important shots.

leading line An element in a composition that leads a viewer's eye toward the subject.

lens flare An effect caused by stray light reflecting off the many glass elements of a lens. Lens shades typically prevent lens glare, but sometimes you can choose to use it creatively by purposely introducing flare into your image.

lighting ratio The proportion between the amount of light falling on the subject from the main light and the secondary light, such as 2:1 — a ratio in which one light is twice as bright as the other.

macro lens A lens with the capability to focus at a very close range, enabling extreme close-up photographs.

manual exposure Bypassing the camera's internal light meter settings in favor of setting the shutter and aperture manually. Manual exposure is beneficial in difficult lighting situations where the camera's meter doesn't provide correct results. When you switch to manual settings, you may need to review a series of photos on the digital camera's LCD to determine the correct exposure.

Matrix metering The Matrix meter (Nikon exclusive) reads the brightness and contrast throughout the entire frame and matches those readings against a database of images (over 30,000 in most Nikon cameras) to determine the best metering pattern to be used to calculate the exposure value.

metering Measuring the amount of light by using a light meter.

NEF (Nikon Electronic File) The name of Nikon's RAW file format.

noise Pixels with randomly distributed color values in a digital image. Noise in digital photographs tends to be more pronounced with low-light conditions and long exposures, particularly when you set your camera to a higher ISO setting.

Noise Reduction (NR) A technology used to decrease the amount of random information in a digital image, often caused by long exposures and high ISO settings.

pincushion distortion A lens aberration in which the lines at the edges and sides of the image are bowed inward. It is usually found in longer focal-length (telephoto) lenses.

Programmed Auto (P) A camera setting where shutter speed and aperture are set automatically.

RAW An image file format that contains the unprocessed camera data as it was captured. Using this format allows you to change image parameters, such as white balance saturation and sharpening. Although you can process RAW files in-camera, the preferred method requires special software, such as Adobe Camera Raw (available in Photoshop), Adobe Lightroom, or Nikon's Capture NX2 or View NX. See also *NEF*.

Rear-curtain sync Rear-curtain sync causes the flash to fire at the end of the exposure an instant before the second, or rear, curtain of the focal plane shutter begins to move. With slow shutter speeds, this feature can create a blur effect from the ambient light, showing as patterns that follow a moving subject, with the subject shown sharply frozen at the end of the blur trail. This setting is usually used in conjunction with longer shutter speeds. See also *Front-curtain sync*.

red-eye An effect from flash photography that appears to make a person's eyes glow red or an animal's yellow or green caused by light bouncing from the retina of the eye. It is most noticeable in dimly lit situations (when the irises are wide open) as well as when the electronic flash is close to the lens and, therefore, prone to reflect the light directly back.

Red-Eye Reduction A Flash mode controlled by a camera setting that's used to prevent the subject's eyes from appearing red in color. The Speedlight fires multiple flashes just before the shutter is opened, with the intention of causing the subject's iris to contract, therefore reflecting less light from the retina to the camera.

self-timer A mechanism that delays the opening of the shutter for several seconds after the Shutter Release button has been pressed.

short lighting When your main light is illuminating the side of the subject that's facing away from you.

shutter A mechanism that allows light to pass to the sensor for a specified amount of time.

Shutter Priority In this camera mode, you set the desired shutter speed and the camera automatically sets the aperture for you. It's best used when you're shooting action shots to freeze the subject's motion by using fast shutter speeds.

shutter speed The length of time the shutter is open to allow light to fall onto the imaging sensor. The shutter speed is measured in seconds or, more commonly, fractions of seconds.

sidelighting Lighting that comes directly from the left or the right of the subject. See also *frontlighting* and *backlighting*.

Single Autofocus (AF-S) A focus setting that locks the focus on the subject when the Shutter Release button is half-pressed. This allows you to focus on the subject and then recompose the image without losing focus as long as the Shutter Release button is half-pressed.

Slow Sync A Flash mode that allows the camera's shutter to stay open for a longer time to allow the ambient light to be recorded. The background receives more exposure, which gives the image a more natural appearance.

Speedlight A Nikon-specific term for its accessory flashes.

spot meter A metering system in which the exposure is based on a small area of the image. On the D3000 the spot is linked to the AF point.

TTL (Through-the-Lens) A metering system where the light is measured directly through the lens.

vanishing point The point at which parallel lines converge and seem to disappear.

Vibration Reduction (VR) A function of the lens in which the lens elements are shifted to reduce the effects of camera shake.

white balance A setting used to compensate for the differences in color temperature from different light sources. For example, a typical tungsten light bulb is very yellow-orange, so the camera adds blue to the image to ensure that the light looks like standard white light.

Index

Index

Index